Primary Teaching Today

An introduction

Denis Hay

Routledge
Taylor & Francis Group

LONDON AND NEW YORK

First published 2009
by Routledge
2 Park Square, Milton Park, Abingdon, Oxon OX14 4RN

Simultaneously published in the USA and Canada
by Routledge
270 Madison Avenue, New York, NY 10016

Routledge is an imprint of the Taylor & Francis Group, an informa business

© 2009 Denis Hayes

Typeset in Bembo by
GreenGate Publishing Services, Tonbridge, Kent

Printed and bound in Great Britain by
CPI Antony Rowe, Chippenham, Wiltshire

British Library Cataloguing in Publication Data
A catalogue record for this book is available from the British Library

Library of Congress Cataloging-in-Publication Data
Hayes, Denis, 1949-
  Primary teaching today : an introduction / Denis Hayes.
    p. cm.
  Includes bibliographical references.
  1. Elementary school teaching--Vocational guidance--Great Britain. 2. Student teaching--Great
Britain. 3. Elementary school teachers--Great Britain. I. Title.
  LB1776.4.G7H38 2008
  372.11020941--dc22
  2008021717

ISBN 10: 0-415-47554-6 (pbk)
ISBN 10: 0-203-88780-8 (ebk)
ISBN 13: 978-0-415-47554-9 (pbk)
ISBN 13: 978-0-203-88780-6 (ebk)

Contents

Part 1

Becoming a primary teacher

Chapter 1

The job you have always dreamed about

The content of Chapter 1 includes:

- a description of the book's purpose
- sources of motivation for teaching
- reference to the principles, implications and application of knowledge
- approaches to the formal education of primary age children
- definitions of a good education.

Points to consider as you read this chapter:

1 The significance of the factors that influenced and continue to influence your desire to teach.
2 Grasping the principles that underpin the use of practical teaching methods and strategies.
3 How to use background knowledge about education systems to shape your views about teaching.
4 Being clear about the overall aims of education and defining success.

The purpose and content of Primary Teaching Today

This book has been written for aspiring student primary teachers – commonly referred to as trainee teachers, student teachers or 'trainees'. It presents the fundamentals of teaching in such a way that you can move forward with greater confidence on three levels:

1 making well-informed choices about the sort of teacher you want to be
2 mastering the skills and strategies that you need to teach effectively
3 satisfying the demands of your training course.

Primary Teaching Today takes you 'behind the scenes' in the classroom and alerts you to the attitudes and practices that all new primary teachers must cultivate to make a success of their work and to gain maximum benefit in doing so. It will be of greatest interest to those who want to teach reception age children (5 year olds) and pupils in key stage 1 (infants; 5–7 year olds; years 1 and 2) and key stage 2 (juniors; 7–11 year olds; years 3, 4, 5 and 6).

The book focuses as much on what teachers should aim to *be* as much as it does on what teachers are meant to *do*. Thus, Part 1 of the book (Becoming a primary teacher) orientates towards the attributes for which beginner teachers should aspire. Part 2 (Teaching and learning) focuses on children and adults working together in the classroom. Part 3 (Trainee teachers on school placement) highlights trainees' experiences in school. Part 4 (Achieving excellence) provides exercises to deepen professional learning, with each exercise linked to the relevant professional Q-Standards required to gain qualified teacher status (QTS) in England and Wales.

Throughout *Primary Teaching Today* there are 'Extend your thinking' prompts that contain statements and questions to stimulate you in facing challenging issues, a 'Terminology check' to clarify meanings of key words and phrases, plus 'Strengthening practice' boxes with practical suggestions about implementation. The 'Professional learning perspectives' at the end of each chapter provide extended quotations and insights from a selection of authors, old and new. The book also contains a number of quotations from the great and the good to stir your imagination and lift your spirits. While it is important to be familiar with what different education writers and theories say about teaching, you must also weigh up the validity of the claims and consider their relevance for practice. These two dimensions (examining authors' claims; considering the relevance for teaching) must work in tandem, such that you examine theories critically in the light of classroom realities.

Terminology check

Trainee teachers (also known as student teachers) are people on a formal course of training that leads to Qualified Teacher Status (QTS).

Professional learning is characterised by formulating, with others, shared values and a vision for education, gaining a better understanding of the way that pupils learn and teachers teach, reflecting constructively on your own classroom practice and that of more experienced colleagues, and sharing your ideas, knowledge and understanding with others.

Motivation for teaching

Perhaps you have always wanted to teach. When you were small your favourite game was pretending to be a teacher, with your friends playing the part of the class. You would sit them down and insist that they attended to what you said. You spoke in a 'teacher voice' and made them answer questions or recite a nursery rhyme or chant a multiplication table. Your friends were normally compliant, unless you asked one to be deliberately naughty, so that you could play at being cross and make them stay in after school. The thrill of those playful experiences has always lingered in your heart. Involvement with voluntary children's groups over the years has only served to reinforce your desire to be a proper teacher.

On the other hand, perhaps you have been working in a different job, becoming increasingly aware of a growing frustration as you contemplate a lifetime of being 'boxed in'. You suddenly realised that you wanted something more fulfilling and absorbing as a career and look towards teaching to provide the answer. Perhaps you have had family responsibilities but your children are now older and you are looking for a change of direction in your life. You have sacrificed a lot for others and feel that it is time to consider your own needs. You have assisted with various child-orientated activities (playgroup, Brownies, parent-helper in school) and found great satisfaction in doing so, but you want something more rewarding, so now it's your turn.

Your life history may be different from any of the above scenarios but you will have one thing in common with almost everyone else who wants to be a teacher, namely, a passionate desire to work with children in school and enjoy the rewards of seeing young lives shaped and transformed because of your influence. Such a prospect drives you on and makes you willing to endure the rigours of the teacher preparation course and the financial and social sacrifices involved. In short, you would do almost anything to fulfil your dream. So here you are. Welcome to dreamland!

Trends in primary education

You are entering teaching at a time of continuous change, much of it for the better, though the majority of time is still spent on the 'core' subjects of mathematics and literacy (English). In May 2003, *Excellence and Enjoyment: A Strategy for Primary Schools* was launched by the Government, setting out the vision for the future of primary education as conveyed through *The Primary National Strategy* (PNS) for literacy (with special attention to speaking and listening) and mathematics. It also incorporated advice and guidance about modern foreign languages (MFL), physical education (PE) and music. Emphasis was placed on the importance of the Arts and using ICT as a means of enhancing learning and teaching. Notably, the PNS emphasises the importance of teachers using tests, targets and tables to help every child develop his or her potential and to measure school performance. *Teachers' TV* was launched in February 2005 with information and resources for teachers, including curriculum-based pro-grammes for use in the classroom.

The *Department for Children, Schools and Families* (DCSF) in England was established in 2007 to promote greater integration between children's services and educational provision, and has already published a lot of material for use in school.[1] In addition to its direct responsibilities, the DCSF is charged with improving children's lives in general, including their health, and alleviating poverty. The attempt to forge closer links between education and other services, and to make schools the hub of the community is leading to changes in the teacher's role. New initiatives include expanding opportunities for physical exer-cise, breakfast clubs and after-school activities, out-of-school extension classes for children deemed in need of additional tuition and homework clubs. The *Every Child Matters* legislation was introduced in 2004 by the DfES (see also Chapter 4 in this book) and given impetus through the Childcare Act (DCSF, 2006). Roche and Tucker (2007) point out that the legislation means that

> teachers will find themselves undertaking different forms of work. As the lead professional they may find themselves working closely with families, especially when it comes to brokering their access to services that are based on school premises … as curriculum opportunities are extended and adult learning is fostered. (p. 220)

It is even possible that with the increasingly close liaison between schools and Children's Centres, you could find yourself teaching in an integrated services' situation which caters for the needs of children and young people from toddler to young adult.

Terminology check

The official publication, *Every Child Matters*, is an approach to the well-being of children and young people from birth to age 19 in which every child, whatever his or her background or circumstances, has support to be healthy, stay safe, enjoy life and achieve, make a positive contribution to society and eventually attain economic security.

In recent years there have also been a number of notable trends in primary pedagogy ('way of teaching') such as whole class teaching in mathematics and

1 In the United Kingdom – consisting of Great Britain and Northern Ireland – the countries of Wales, Scotland and Northern Ireland have separate decision-making bodies for (amongst other things) education. Consequently, their education policies differ in some respects from those in England.

the use of so-called 'synthetic' phonics for teaching children to read (see Johnston and Watson, 2007). Curriculum changes in England have encouraged teachers to focus more closely on individual pupil needs and creative forms of teaching, rather than being constrained by statutory requirements. PE in school has made something of a 'come-back' owing to concerns about childhood obesity, supported by a number of national and local healthy-eating initiatives. The use of Information Technology in teaching and recording pupil progress has had a major impact on practice, though not, perhaps, the wholesale transformation that Government envisaged. Global and environmental awareness has also been actively promoted in schools, with particular emphasis on the impact of climate change. Sadly, societal trends have also made it necessary to educate primary children about sexual responsibility (as part of the science curriculum) and provide information about drug misuse. Most schools have adopted a curriculum resource and framework for promoting the social and emotional aspects of learning (known as SEAL) through self-awareness, managing feelings, motivation, empathy and social skills.

Terminology check

The word *curriculum* is used in five ways:

1   prescribed programmes of work
2   the range of academic and social knowledge with which children engage in school
3   the pursuit of knowledge and understanding outside the regular curriculum
4   the implicit ('implied') learning priorities of a teacher or school
5   the content of tests.

Scotland has its own distinctive and flexible qualification framework that is separate from the National Curriculum framework used in England, Wales and Northern Ireland. Scotland's curriculum is divided into the 5–14 Curriculum, and the Standard Grade for 14–16 year olds. It is not set by law and places considerable responsibility on local authorities and schools to deliver a good service. The 5–14 Curriculum is divided into six attainment levels, graded from A to F, and assessments of pupils' attainment is taken by individuals or groups when the teacher considers appropriate. The curriculum in Wales places greater emphasis on teacher assessment of children's progress and, unlike England, does not publish league tables of national test results in the primary phase, school by school.

So you are entering the profession at a time when salaries have increased, working conditions improved and there is official support for teachers using their ingenuity and imagination to make learning more exciting and relevant for the children. And after all, isn't that what teachers were always *supposed* to do?

Extend your thinking

Being creative requires discipline, the development of skills and good judgement. It should not be confused with haphazardness.

Terminology check

Learning can be defined in four ways:

1 learning something factual (knowledge)
2 learning about something (understanding)
3 learning how to do something (skills)
4 learning to be someone (attitude).

Being professional

Professional teachers – unlike amateurs and well doers – don't just 'deliver' a curriculum; they understand pupil learning, child development, education theory and how to apply their knowledge in practical teaching, as well as being skilled in relating to adults. It is helpful to think of the professional role in consisting of three dimensions:

1 Establishing the *key principles* of education involved.
2 Exploring their *implications for practice*.
3 Looking at ways in which the principle and its implications apply to a particular situation ('the context'); that is, examining the *application*.

It is sometimes the case that advice offered in books and from tutors/teachers start with the application and neglect dealing with the principles and implications. One of the most common examples of this unhelpful tendency to 'look through the wrong end of the telescope' is in the area of behaviour and discipline. If, say, children are working noisily, you may be advised to use various strategies that provide an 'instant solution' to the problem; for instance:

• Hold your hand up in the air as a signal that all the children should stop talking.
• Write the names of noisy children on the board.

- Ask the children to stop their work, stand up or put their fingers on lips.
- Shake a tambourine.

These techniques are valid and commonly used in class; however, if you deal solely with this 'application' element without understanding the principles and implications, you will be acting more as a technician (i.e. somebody possessing a set of techniques) rather than as an educator. Even in instances where you spontaneously react to a situation in class, an essential element of being a professional is to reflect later on what you have done and ask searching questions about its significance and appropriateness. For instance, in the above example of children working noisily, you may create the following schema:

Principle: Children work more effectively in a calm atmosphere.
Implication: When the noise level rises, children must be taught to respond appropriately to a given signal from the teacher.
Application: Children will be encouraged to speak softly and concentrate on their own work.

A little thought about the above schema should alert you to the fact that even when working from broad principle to specific practice there is a need to use your classroom experiences to modify and refine the original principle and its implications. Thus, it is frequently beneficial for pupils to work quietly but there are instances where conversation and even raised voices are appropriate and important for learning. For example, if children are debating a topic or experimenting with equipment it is obviously appropriate to do so by talking about issues or procedures and not by miming or using hand signals. Again, drama or a physical session may invite the deliberate use of strident tones, commands or calling out. As a result you may wish to modify the schema to read something like this:

Principle: Children normally work more effectively in a calm atmosphere.
Implication: When the noise level rises, children must be taught to respond appropriately to a given signal from the teacher.
Application: When working singly, children will be encouraged to speak softly and concentrate on their own work; when working together, children may speak more forcibly, as directed by the teacher.

You may have noticed that the principle has been modified by the addition of the adverb 'normally' and the schema's wording now acknowledges that there is a need for the teacher to exercise greater discretion about noise levels as dictated by particular circumstances. Of course you may design a wholly different set of statements from those suggested above. The important point is that you actively interrogate your actions (and those of others) and use the principle/implication/application format as a means of thinking carefully, not only about what is done but also why it is done. This approach will help you to avoid making an artificial division between theory and practice, as, in reality, the relationship is a much more dynamic one.

Extend your thinking

Avoid adopting positions in which you:

- claim that you can only learn by practical experience of 'what works'
- implement ideas without questioning their deeper meaning
- do something because it is recommended in a book or official publication.

The well-educated child

You want to be a teacher, but what do you want to *teach* the children? No doubt you intend to show them how to read and write well, to do sums and master other dimensions of mathematics, to learn about their immediate and wider world and eventually to succeed in their exams. I hope you also want to introduce them to the wonders of art, construction, music, dance, games and poetry, and influence your pupils such that they grow up to be decent, well-adjusted people who make positive contributions to society. You might see your role as something of a moral mentor in assisting children to negotiate a safe passage through the vagaries of life's experiences and to make sensible choices and decisions. In all likelihood, you see the work of a teacher as an amalgam of all these parts: academic, personal and social, in helping to produce a *well-educated child*.

It is far from simple to define 'a well-educated child' but it is important to spend time considering what it means or you might fall into the trap of confusing it with 'getting good test results'. Although test scores are important, they only form an element of a far more complex set of aspirations for children, incorporating self-confidence, empathy, a willingness to struggle beyond the comfort zone and a desire to probe and find solutions to intractable problems. A well-educated child will possess knowledge about herself or himself (what I think and why I think it), about the world in which she or he lives (interrogating the things we take for granted) and the history that has led us to do the things we do and behave in the way we behave (our cultural heritage). Alongside this sort of knowledge, the well-educated child will also be developing attitudes that shape his or her view of learning, seeking out and absorbing new information at every opportunity and discovering innovative ways to apply it. Crucially, the child will possess the communication and interpersonal skills that are necessary to speak and write clearly, effectively and persuasively. In the modern world, communicating electronically has also assumed great importance, though concerns have been expressed about its excessive use at the expense of more traditional methods – particularly the reduction in face-to-face encounters and 'hands-on' experiences.

Over time, a well-educated child will learn to collaborate with others, listen to their ideas respectfully and thoughtfully, and accept or reject them on the basis of clear and logical thinking, as well as drawing on previous practical experiences of similar situations. He or she will develop the analytical skills needed to solve problems, make sound decisions and reflect values that show tolerance and respect for cultural, ethnic and intellectual diversity. People who are endowed with such qualities are not the 'anything goes' or 'live and let live' types; on the contrary, they are thoroughly decent human beings who may not excel in everything they do and sometimes have to struggle and persevere to achieve what their more illustrious peers take for granted, but contribute positively to society and genuinely seek to be a responsible person. These sentiments are not fluffy fantasies for idealists; on the contrary, they are essential attributes for a peaceful society and contented nation. I'm sure you agree that we urgently need them.

Extend your thinking

Children are not poor, weak and helpless: they are capable of achieving heights of excellence; of gaining powerful insights into complex issues; and of performing amazing feats of creativity. But they need your support, guidance and affirmation as they seek to do so.

Defining success

If you teach very young children, you may feel rather alarmed by some of the suggestions offered above about a well-educated child. For instance, can we really expect a five year old to show tolerance and respect and defend an ethical position? In answering such concerns, it is important to acknowledge two key points. First, if we don't aspire to these aims, it is unlikely that they will be achieved. Second, there is no end point in being well educated; it is a process that should continue throughout life. Your responsibility and privilege is to help to establish a framework – stressing positive attitudes and appropriate behaviour (attitude to self and towards others) – within which useful knowledge, skills and understanding can be nurtured and promoted. Parents, friends and societal pressures will ultimately determine the extent and vigour of the growth in each individual, but you play an integral part in creating the right conditions for it to occur.

We all want our pupils to succeed, but defining success is far from easy. General definitions might include statements such as, 'when things turn out as well or better than expected', 'achieving what you aim to do', or 'growing, developing, improving and getting better'. Pupils in school often equate success with the pleasant and powerful feeling of getting good grades, ticks on a page, commending comments or tangible rewards such as stickers and house points. Some children find fulfilment in completing a piece of academic work; others in solving practical tasks; yet others in sealing and affirming personal friendships. In fact, all of these elements are important and part of your job is to help children to appreciate that inner happiness and contentment can be created through small achievements: a letter shape correctly made for the first time; a thoughtful answer to a question; a valid contribution to a discussion; a helpful comment to a classmate; a creative and imaginative response to a task; perseverance in tracking down information, and so forth. In other words, success is not confined to the major events of life but is regularly located in the workaday world of school life. It is for this reason that adults need to be alert to opportunities for commending seemingly ordinary achievements and convincing children that they really have accomplished something worthwhile. These principles are valid for the criteria you apply to your *own* success, too!

Acknowledging success

Pupils are successful if they:

- do something to be proud of
- achieve something for the first time
- persevere with a difficult task to completion
- finish an onerous piece of work without complaining
- receive the admiration of classmates
- behave wisely at a crucial moment
- lead and guide others
- gain a high mark in a test
- exceed expectations in completing a task
- transfer their knowledge to a new situation
- remain positive despite setbacks and problems.

Extend your thinking

Enjoyment of school drops with age from about 90 per cent of children at the start of primary school to about 70 per cent at the end. What factors might influence the change in attitude and how can you help?

Professional learning perspectives

Education is about morality as well as intellect

Nel Noddings (1992) argues that different people have different strengths and that these strengths should be cultivated in an environment of caring, not of competition. She insists that intimate relations provide an essential climate for effective learning, in which the teacher's role is crucially significant. Furthermore, Noddings claims that all pupils should be engaged in

> a general education that guides them in caring for self, intimate others, global others, plants, animals and the environment, the human-made world and ideas. Moral life so defined should be frankly embraced as the main goal of education. Such an aim does not work against intellectual development or academic achievement; on the contrary, it supplies a firm foundation for both. (p. 174)

The purpose of education must be defined first

Alfie Kohn (2003) submits the following perspective on education:

> Rather than attempting to define what it means to be well educated, should we instead be asking about the *purposes of education* [plural]? The latter formulation invites us to look beyond academic goals ... to reject the deadly notion that the school's first priority should be intellectual development and contends that the main aim of education should be to produce competent, caring, loving and lovable people. Alternatively, we might wade into the dispute between those who see education as a means to creating or sustaining a democratic society and those who believe its primary role is *economic*, amounting to an 'investment' in future workers and, ultimately, corporate profits. In short, perhaps the question, *'How do we know if education has been successful?'* shouldn't be posted until we have asked what it is supposed to be successful at [doing]. (p. 6)

Not all success is measurable

The late Robert (Bobby) Kennedy, US Senator and brother of President John Kennedy, spoke about the folly of only using measurable outcomes to judge success. Thus:

> Gross National Product measures neither the health of our children, the quality of their education, nor the joy of their play. It measures neither the beauty of our poetry nor the strength of our marriages. It is indifferent to the decency of our factories and the safety of our streets alike. It measures neither our wisdom nor our learning, neither our wit nor our courage,

neither our compassion nor our devotion to our country. It measures everything, in short, except that which makes life worth living. It can tell us everything about our country except those things that make us proud to be a part of it. (Speech, Ball State University, 4 April 1968)

Find out more by reading

Noddings, N. (2005) *Happiness and Education*, Cambridge: Cambridge University Press.
Richards, C. (ed.) (2001) *Changing English Primary Education*, Stoke-on-Trent: Trentham.

Chapter 2

The realities of teaching

The content of Chapter 2 includes:

- testimonies from trainee teachers about their experiences in school
- understanding schools and teachers
- contributing to the educative process
- behind the scenes of a teacher's day
- the inter-relatedness and complexity of the teacher's role.

Points to consider as you read this chapter:

1 How to face the emotional, intellectual and physical challenges attached to teaching.
2 Defining qualities of the best teachers.
3 Finding out from serving teachers about the realities of the job.

Trainee teachers in school

When trainee teachers are asked about their experiences in school, most of them positively glow with pride about their achievements, a small percentage regret they had ever chosen to teach; the majority admit to a mixture of uplifting and of challenging times. There is general agreement among all teachers that even though working in school is difficult, emotionally draining and exhausting, the job is eminently worthwhile. Being immersed in an environment with children is tiring, exhilarating and edifying, sometimes all at the same time, but few would seriously consider doing anything else. The mixture of emotions is well expressed by one trainee teacher in her diary:

> I enjoyed my time in school even though it was hectic and I think I came home some days feeling really daunted with what I'm going to have to do

here. I was surprised how different it could be from my last school placement in the way that things were organised and the kind of way the work
was done with the children as well. This is going to take quite a bit of getting used to! I felt exhausted actually; I'd forgotten how tired I get. I did
enjoy it, but some days were better than others.

People who are quietly cynical about the work done by teachers and half-
believe the maxim that *those who can't, teach*, as George Bernard Shaw famously
claimed, have obviously never had to deal with young children, day in, day out.
In fact, one of the greatest thrills of the job is to see the fulfilment that successful teaching and learning engenders in pupils. It really is true that happy
teachers produce happy children who enthuse about learning; similarly, happy
children produce happy teachers who want to go on exploring and discovering
how to do their work better.

Terminology check

Training provider is the official title given to the institution or body that is
responsible for your training course that leads to QTS. Other postgraduate
routes into teaching involve a continuous placement at the same school.

Understanding schools and teachers

Schools have many routines and processes embedded in their daily practice that
are not evident to the outsider but quickly become apparent when someone
begins to work there. There are traditions, conventions, professional disputes,
personality tensions, bureaucratic procedures, implicit and explicit pedagogies
and a tangle of well-considered and instinctive responses to situations to which
the newcomer is gradually exposed. The world of teaching requires determination and the ability to think 'on your feet', as you respond to an endless flow of
children's questions and make decisions with knowledge, care and wisdom.
The myth that becoming a good teacher depends on finding the 'holy grail' of
practice – aided, abetted and sometimes hindered by advice from people who
do not work in your classroom with your pupils but claim to have all the
answers – fails to do justice to the difficult task that those charged with the
education of our children have to face daily. The joys and perils of being a
primary teacher await you, so come on in, the water's fine!

You will gather that teaching is not the smooth, seamless robe that official
documents present as normal and achievable. Pupil learning is often messy,
unpredictable and difficult to assess formally. Despite the fact that shelves are
groaning with the weight of numerous publications alleging to help us to
understand the educative process, the truth is that teachers mainly rely on

a 'sixth sense' to guide their actions, honed through months and years of direct experience with children.

Teachers also use a bank of positive strategies to reinforce behaviour and shape class discipline, supported by rewards, sanctions and punishments agreed by the staff and written into a policy document. However, a policy is only a guideline and not a blueprint for action; over and above the formal requirements, you have to be the final arbiter of what is appropriate in any given situation. It is in the minutiae of the moment by moment 'lived experience' as a teacher that principles of teaching and learning are worked out. It is the way that each teacher *exercises* her or his judgement to implement the requirements that distinguishes the effective practitioner from the merely efficient one.

The best example of the truth that it is teachers rather than systems that make the essential difference to pupil learning is seen when a class is shared between two teachers. The first teacher is abrupt, unsmiling and regularly finds things to moan about. Pupils are compliant and subdued. They complete the tasks and work feverishly, ever conscious of the teacher's steely glare and uncompromising stance. Lunchtime comes as a welcome relief.

The second teacher arrives a little later, full of smiles, chatting to the children, greedily absorbing their news and brimming with life. She is aware of the children's carefully coded criticisms of the morning teacher but studiously avoids being drawn into a discussion. The children work enthusiastically for her, if a little noisily, and strive to achieve their best. They are sometimes mischievous but think too highly of their teacher to take unreasonable advantage. Anyway, they know that she can be fiercely uncompromising if pushed too far. When school ends the children skip from the classroom, their minds full of the learning experiences they have recently enjoyed; they cannot wait to tell their friends, siblings and people at home about what they have been doing.

The first teacher is full of jargon and endlessly quotes from government circulars to her colleagues. The second teacher makes sure that bureaucracy serves the children, and not the other way around. The first teacher is largely concerned with policy implementation; the second teacher wants principles to precede practice. The first teacher is admired and gets results in measurable ways; the second teacher is loved and gets results in measurable *and* immeasurable ways, such as fostering determination, perseverance, support for others, an encouraging attitude and a willingness to accept temporary failure to achieve lasting success. Which teacher do you think is more likely to assist the children to develop their thinking, creativity, passion for learning and thirst for knowledge? Which teacher will produce well-educated pupils? Yes, I think so, too! See also Chapter 3.

Your contribution to the process

You may have read this far and wonder if, with the many and various demands made of teachers, you can ever reach the necessary standard. After all, you are just a beginner, a novice, a fledgling still struggling to fly and prove yourself to your assessors – tutors, class teachers and mentors. You may not have even begun formal training and only have voluntary experiences to guide your thinking. In fact, while it is true that you are new and inexperienced, you also have more knowledge and ability than you might realise. Naturally, the host teachers and assistants possess insights and skills that you are still perfecting but that fact should not make you feel that you are a mere appendage in the teaching process. For instance, you may be better equipped to deal with technological aids than your hosts. Furthermore, in addition to the present training course, your past experience as a teaching assistant, nursery nurse, parent helper or leader of a children's community project offers that most precious of all assets, namely, the ability to think logically, consult with others, accommodate a spectrum of different opinions, evaluate options, organise events and manage complexity.

Once you are caught up in the maelstrom of regular planning, teaching, assessing and the plethora of other responsibilities that qualified teachers undertake (break duties, reports, staff meeting, clubs, parent evenings and so on) it is difficult to step back and take stock of what you are doing and why. Consequently, it is essential to make good use of the requirement attached to every training course that you must evaluate your teaching and set targets for improving practice. The major benefit of adopting such a reflective approach is rooted in the *thinking* that you undertake, as much as the formal recording of your ideas.

Terminology check

Reflection involves 'taking a step back' from a situation, considering the relevant factors that impact upon it and evaluating the implications for practice.

Teaching can be and sometimes is a frustrating, tiresome and unappealing job. Every teacher has moments when she or he wants to throw in the towel and find a simpler way to earn a living. Nevertheless, it *is* possible to be a successful, happy teacher with successful, happy children, as thousands of primary practitioners have shown down the years. And you can be among them. Read on to find out how.

Extend your thinking

What gets you out of bed in the morning?

- the thought of working with children
- working with colleagues
- pleasing my tutor

- fear of the consequences if I don't
- to get qualified
- to pay the bills.

How does your motivation influence your attitude?

Behind the scenes in a teacher's day

Teachers work hard and the true nature of teachers' work and the variety of skills required for the job can be daunting. But what is the 'daily grind' like for teachers? To give you insights into the practical and emotional dimensions of the job, let me introduce you to Don (pseudonym), who teaches in a medium-sized inner-city primary school with a diverse intake and kept a detailed record of just one day in his working life. By looking closely at Don's day, it soon becomes obvious that the role of the primary teacher is complex, sometimes contradictory, and not capable of being managed in the smooth, predictable and dispassionate way that the recent emphasis on competencies, standards and target setting implies. The information that follows is accurate but has been shaped into a narrative style to increase readability.

Don's diary

7.50 a.m. I set out from home around 7.30 a.m., park my car on the edge of town and cycle in the rest of the way to school. Several staff vehicles are already in the car park.

8.10 a.m. I go to my room to make final preparations for the maths session that follows the assembly, ensuring that the number arrow cards are intact and switching on my laptop computer. Then I check the notes I left for myself on Friday, write the date on the whiteboard, leave myself a bold reminder about collecting in the homework and put a registration activity on the board to keep the class occupied during the first few frantic minutes of the day. I place their English books in neat piles on the various tables so that the children can put them away in their trays when they arrive. I suddenly remember that I've got to photocopy some work sheets I devised last night as an extension task for the more able children, so I hurry off to the resources room to get it done. I'd like to ask my TA to do the job but she hasn't arrived yet.

8.25 a.m. I spend over five minutes queuing to use the machine and wishing that I'd done the job last week. I hurriedly check my pigeonhole and find two letters that have to be given to pupils in my class and a revised contact list of addresses and telephone numbers to be confirmed with the children during registration. Lizzy, the newly qualified teacher for whom I am the mentor ('induction tutor'), asks if she can speak to me sometime today, 'when you are not too busy', and we arrange to meet during the lunch break. I think she wants some feedback from a lesson I observed last Thursday. I can hardly believe that we still haven't had a proper chance to sit down and discuss things since then.

8.45 a.m. I go to the playground to gather up my class. A parent tells me that her son has pulled a muscle and needs to be excused from PE. She hurries away before I think to ask her for a confirmatory letter. Another parent tells me that she's anxious that an older child might have been bullying her daughter. I tell her to pop along and see me after school this evening. I also make a mental note that I must (once again) talk to the girl involved about it. The mother explains to me that she can't come tonight as she's working but that she'll call in later in the week. It's only after she's gone that I remember that I shall be away on a course on Wednesday and Thursday. After saying hello to various children and enthusing about the bits of news they share with me, I try to focus my thoughts on the morning ahead. My mind is buzzing already.

8.50 a.m. The whistle sounds for a second time and children continue to line up. I greet my class but they are quite restless and my voice drifts away into the open spaces as I call them to order. I keep a special eye on Ryan to see if he has taken his medication to calm his aggression, and, also, on Paul to make sure he isn't picking on the smaller children again. Tara is desperate to tell me about the family wedding she went to at the weekend. I try to sound interested while keeping things orderly as we make our way into the building and out of the drenching rain that has begun to fall. The class seems noisier than usual and the sound echoes eerily down the corridor. As the children scurry around hanging up coats, putting lunch boxes away and chattering into the classroom, I hear myself complaining loudly about the din, but merely succeed in adding to the cacophony. Ruby creeps close to me and confides in a breathless whisper that Aston has brought a penknife to school, so I ask him directly if it is true. He nods and produces it nonchalantly, insisting that he 'weren't gonna use it'. I ask him to give it to me and he hands it over at once.

8.55 a.m. I ask the TA, Mrs Pompay, who has just arrived at school, to keep an eye on things for me while I race up to the office with the contraband penknife and quickly explain to the head teacher, Mrs Mandrake, what has happened. I hurry back to my classroom and reprimand George and Ben who are busy scampering around the cloakroom. Arthur, as usual, stands aloof and silent. I wonder what sort of experience he has had, coping with yet another adult male presence in the tiny house he shares with his immature mother and four sisters. I make a note of the fact that Ryan is already looking and sounding extremely lively, give out the two notes from the secretary, begin to call the register and check the lunch arrangements; at least I don't have to collect dinner money like we used to do. The classroom assistant from next door pops her head around the door to tell me that Mrs Young, who normally gives Ryan and two other children additional support with their work, has had to stay at home to nurse her poorly child. My heart sinks as I face the prospect of having to cope with Ryan all morning.

9.03 a.m. I talk briefly to the children about the weekend's homework and remind them to complete their diaries. Cheng immediately tells me he has left his work at home (again). Amy looks at me blankly. I don't press the matter with her as she has had more than enough to put up with from angry adults in her short life. I collect up the homework and make a few general comments about it, though not many of them seem to be listening. Ben asks if they have to do the 'early work' off the board. I had completely forgotten about it but reply rather stiffly that 'yes, of course' they must do it. They seem relieved to have something to concentrate on. I breathe a little more easily.

9.10 a.m. The class settles and I watch their bent forms over the tables, with knotted brows, pencils tapping on chins, sudden gleams and gasps of inspiration, discrete copying and vacant stares. Time melts away until Petra asks whether we should be on our way to assembly yet. Now it's my turn to gasp as I gather the class together and march them down to the hall, uttering a variety of pleas for them to 'be more sensible' as we seem to take forever to cover the short distance. The echoing silence from other classrooms as we pass them confirms that we are late. We burst rather unceremoniously into the hall and the head gives me one of her 'we have all been waiting for you' stares. I try a weak smile of apology and find a vacant chair, trying to look inconspicuous. A few of my colleagues glance across the hall sympathetically. It's so frustrating that the head insists on having an assembly so early in the week, but she argues that it helps to foster a sense of unity. After a few minutes I notice that Ryan has started to shuffle forward towards some other mischievous boys in a different class, so I get him to sit by my feet.

9.30 a.m. Assembly comes to an end. I take the children back to the classroom and send them off to their different mathematics groups. This is always a messy time, with bodies moving in different directions, opening and shutting of trays and occasional collisions, prompting the inevitable recriminations as children find their way to the correct room. I spend the next few minutes organising, helping to find missing books and shepherding those who can't remember what they should be doing or where they should be going.

9.35 a.m. The confusion quickly passes and I gather my group around me and begin the maths lesson that will run for the next 50 minutes or so. I enjoy the stimulus of the question-and-answer (mental maths) phase. We rehearse some of the key points from previous lessons and I introduce the tasks; the children are soon busy working. I find this interactive and creative format so much more fulfilling than a rigidly structured lesson. The children apply themselves with a will and I begin to feel more relaxed and satisfied after the wobbly start to the day.

10.30 a.m. The children come back from their different groups, jostling for a place so that they can return their books to their trays. I send the children out for their break, only to discover that it's a 'wet playtime' and they have to stay inside. Several of the boys stand there with a football and insist that they don't mind getting wet; they look disappointed and genuinely puzzled when I tell them that they are not allowed to run around in the rain. This change of plan complicates the preparation for the literacy session to follow, as I normally use part of the break time to set out resources, liaise with the TA and mentally think through the lesson (a strategy I have tried to use since college days). However, I manage to put away the mathematics equipment, check the computer to make sure that the film sequence I'm going to show them later is okay and get my materials in order. I dash to the staff room and grab a quick drink, share a few bits of gossip with colleagues and ask the trainee teacher how she's coping with her class. About two minutes later, the knock at the door ushers in several shy children, each hugging an empty tea mug and giving the unwelcome news that it is now 'in time'. I pour my half-finished coffee down the sink and rush off to the classroom, remembering as I do so that I was supposed to telephone a colleague in a nearby school about organising a football match. It will just have to wait.

10.50 a.m. I spend the first few minutes after break making the children sort out the mess that has accumulated. Games are put away, half-finished drawings gathered up and furniture re-organised. Ben and Ahmed are trying to resolve a disagreement (with Ryan as referee) and Sally is quietly weeping in the book corner. Sally often cries and it's hard to know when it's a serious matter and when it's not. Thankfully, Mrs Pompay is dealing with the matter.

10.55 a.m. The children gather on the carpet and the literacy session begins. As we read the text in unison, I notice that at least three children are not saying anything, but merely opening and shutting their mouths like goldfish, so we start again and I proceed more slowly. I spend some time revising the vocabulary and rehearsing some of the phrases. When I ask them, the children say that they understand my explanation about using speech marks. I am not at all certain that they do but press on anyway as the clock glares down at me from the wall. As the group work commences, a few children go out for additional support. Thankfully, due to Mrs Young's enforced absence, the pupils needing extra help are combining with the group working with Mrs Hooper, the learning-support assistant from the parallel class. She will certainly have her hands full. Ryan has stayed fairly calm so far this morning but he is capable of erratic behaviour.

11.55 a.m. The literacy lesson finishes and, is it my imagination, or do all the children sigh with relief? I particularly regret the limited opportunity we have to do extended writing. The fragmented nature of the session leaves me little room for manoeuvre and I feel that I need to break free and be more imaginative with the time. Perhaps it's my creative streak or maybe I'm more like Ryan than I care to admit! The recent changes to the curriculum mean that we should have more flexibility over how we teach in future; I certainly hope so.

12 noon. After some initial problems sorting out the computer, I show the class a short history film extract about Ancient Egypt as a 'taster' for what we are going to study. I briefly introduce the tasks that we will tackle tomorrow in the main History session and give them a simple task for homework about finding out the age of the oldest and youngest person from among their family and friends. Some of them get quite excited and the morning ends with a buzz. They seem to be genuinely interested and their enthusiasm cheers me up.

12.20 p.m. Lunchtime arrives. I dismiss the class, tidy away my bits and pieces, then go to the science store to collect the resource boxes for 'Light' and some prisms for the experiments this afternoon. I set them out along the window ledges for easy access. On checking the work cards, I discover that two of them have been damaged and need to be written out again. The school administrator pops her head around the door and asks if I have remembered to check the new revised contact list. I confess that I haven't but promise to do so tomorrow. She smiles and says that it's not a problem, but I know it must be a nuisance for her. Half a minute later, Mrs Mandrake also looks around the door to tell me that she had contacted Aston's mother about the penknife.

1.00 p.m. I eat my lunch while having a meeting with Lizzy about the mathematics session I had observed some days before. I apologise again for the fact that we haven't met to discuss the lesson in detail but plead that I have genuinely been up to my ears in work. She smiles and says that it's not a problem – she's the second person to say that to me in the past couple of minutes – but I know that she's frustrated about having to wait for feedback and I can hardly blame her. Where does the time go once you step inside school? I'm aware of the two trainee teachers on placement sitting nearby, soaking up my every word as I talk to Lizzy, while pretending not to listen. It's easy to forget all the pressures associated with being a student and I find myself smiling warmly at them.

1.15 p.m. I begin to relax into an easy chair and to chat to my colleague about the field trip we are planning, but the meal-time assistant (MTA) brings a young child called Jenny to me (as a first aid person) to check her bumped and bleeding head because the playground supervisor who normally deals with such incidents is off sick. I can't find the box of disposable gloves, so I do without them and try to reassure the anxious child while carefully inspecting the wound. It looks ugly, so I leave her with the MTA while I ask the secretary to contact the parent. I scribble some details in the accident book and spend several minutes tracking down the class teacher to inform her of the situation. She promises to sort it out.

1.20 p.m. I race outside to find that all the other classes have gone inside and mine is waiting impatiently for me. Katie complains that Ethan called her a name; he denies it vehemently but it's probably true. I hurry them along to the classroom and hear myself speaking rather sharply to them again. It's not a good start to the afternoon but I console myself that events have conspired against me and it is just one of those days. I don't intend to allow myself to slip into the role of 'Mr Nasty' just because I can't organise my time better.

1.30 p.m. After spending a short time trying to reconcile two tearful friends who have fallen out during the lunch break, we begin the science lesson. A child reminds me that I haven't taken the register, so there is a pause while it's done, made worse by the unexpected arrival of children selling poppies. Some five minutes later I settle the children and re-start the lesson. In my hurry to make up for lost time, I completely forget my usual practice of telling the children what we are doing and why, inviting them to ask questions, and so forth. Instead, I get them down to work on the practical tasks as quickly as possible and circulate in a less interactive manner than normal. The children are restlessly excited and I'm thankful that my lesson is not being observed by an inspector or a colleague. I retain my slightly aloof manner with the children until the end of the practical phase as a means of calming the situation. The children remain unaware of my concerns and are having immense fun; even Ryan is talking about the work and dishing out suggestions about how to do things to his friends. I feel much better again.

2.25 p.m. The practical part of the lesson ends and the children tidy away their science equipment with surprising efficiency. I commend them for doing so and the atmosphere lightens further. We spend a couple of minutes discussing the outcomes and I explain the way the work is to be written up. Ryan asks me in a depressed tone why we always have to write about the experiment. I tell him all about the use of writing frames but he isn't interested. I hear him whisper to nobody in particular that 'writing is rubbish' but I decide to ignore the remark. I work with the lower ability children and it appears to go reasonably smoothly, though the process seems to be uncomfortably like the stereotypical science 'write-ups' I did at secondary school. Perhaps Ryan is right and we should spend less time writing and more time enjoying the enquiry-based element of the work, celebrating our discoveries and discussing the implications.

3.05 p.m. The children hand in their work and we tidy up the room. I read them a couple of humorous poems to finish the day. In my weary state, they don't seem as funny as usual but the children, pleased to be relieved of formal work for a short time, laugh freely and keep asking for another one.

3.20 p.m. School ends. I send the children home and follow them through to the playground, as I want to catch the mother of a new boy from Japan who cannot speak English and communicates a lot using sign language. The mother smiles and nods but I'm not sure that she understands what I'm saying. I also have a talk with two girls about some playground incidents that have been reported to me. I explain that I don't want to hear any more about their spiteful remarks and that I expect them to be kind to the other children. They feign innocence and claim that it was the other children's fault. I notice that they exchange sly smiles as they walk out through the gate, so I shall have to keep an eye on them. Meena's father strides across to me, beaming as usual, and thanks me (not for the first time) for the lovely work his daughter is doing and how much he appreciates my efforts on her behalf. Parents like him are such a joy.

3.40 p.m. As I return to the classroom, I notice that three children who are picked up by taxi are still waiting for their lift. I can't find the head or deputy, and the administrator has had to leave early, so I tell the children to sit in the lobby while I telephone the company to report the problem. After several fruitless minutes trying to get an answer, I go back to the lobby to ask the children if they have any ideas about what has gone wrong, but they are not there so I panic and wonder what has happened to them. I begin to hunt around the school when Anne, the reception class teacher, calls across to me and asks if I am looking for the taxi children because, if I am, they have just gone off in the car. A wave of relief flushes my head and I feel like hugging her. Instead I reply casually that although I was looking for them it can wait until tomorrow, but thank her anyway. I don't intend to disclose my irrational emotional turmoil to her!

3.55 p.m. I wander back to my room, tidy my desk, take the science equipment back to the store and begin to pin up some children's work on the display board. As I do so, I realise (to my shame) that it has been largely empty since the start of term. I must discuss it with the TA tomorrow. I glance at the record-sheets with all the 'tracking' of progress information that we are supposed to complete by the end of the week but I can't face doing them at the moment. I remember that I've arranged a meeting with my colleague, Elaine, about the museum trip we are organising for the end of the month and my heart sinks as I remember that I still haven't telephoned the teacher about the football match. I hurry to the telephone, only to find that it is engaged. Elaine is nowhere to be found, so I conclude (thankfully) that she must have forgotten about our arrangement and got involved in something else.

4.10 p.m. The caretaker and I discuss the problem with a carpet that is lifting up in the classroom and becoming quite hazardous. He says that he will see what he can do. I know that I can rely on him to get something sorted out one way or another. I check the gymnastic equipment in the store ahead of tomorrow's session, nodding an apology to my colleague, Ben, who is in the hall conducting the first choir rehearsal for Christmas, even though it's only the first week of November.

4.25 p.m. I decide to do something that will feel like useful work, so I clean the board, put tomorrow's date, an outline of the daily plan and some 'early work'. At least we don't have assembly first thing in the morning.

4.40 p.m. I make myself a cup of coffee, chat briefly to the deputy about his forthcoming headship interview, exchange a word with the trainees and make my way back to the classroom to mark the science write-ups they did during the afternoon. I do the job as fast as possible, putting a large number of ticks and commending comments, even though the majority of the work is mundane. I hope that my positive approach will encourage the children and motivate them to try harder next time.

5.05 p.m. I collect up the mathematics work to mark at home, my planning file to finish off the details for the RE I'm teaching to Year 6 tomorrow and my record-folder to tick off a few more pages of concepts that the children have supposedly grasped. I am also determined to finish the reports for the parents' evening.

5.30 p.m. I'm tired and need to get home but after the problems of this morning I decide to download two pages for shared text work for tomorrow's literacy work. It also occurs to me that I haven't found out whether Mrs Young, the classroom assistant with the sick child, will be in school tomorrow.

5.40 p.m. I scribble myself a list of 'essential' things to do tomorrow. It looks ominously long. I fetch my bike from the shed in the growing darkness and, at 5.50 p.m. cycle out of school to the place where I have parked my car. As I weave my way gingerly through the rush hour traffic, I feel thankful that although today has been demanding and I haven't had much of a chance to stop and relax, at least we did not have a staff meeting.

6.35 p.m. I arrive home and stagger thankfully into the house. My children come to greet me but catch the exhausted look in my eyes and retreat to wait for a better moment. My wife gives me a reproving look, reminding me that we have an appointment at our son's parents' evening at 7 p.m. I had forgotten about it in the busyness of the day. My tea will have to wait until after the appointment is over.

Postscript: The marking, files, record-folders and draft reports sit sternly in my bag, demanding attention. They are still untouched when, weary but determined, I get up at 6.30 a.m. the following morning. How it is that I still love this crazy, wonderful job, I simply do not know!

Demands on teachers

The account of Don's day underlines the extreme busyness and diversity that characterises a teacher's day in school and the many demands placed upon Don can usefully be described under the following headings.

Intensity

Don's day was characterised by the pace of life, limited opportunity for thoughtful reflection and the need to prioritise tasks. He was obliged to perform some tasks 'on the hoof' as he coped with a variety of distractions and diversions. Teachers need to develop the skill of making instant decisions about the significance of different demands and how they should deal with them.

Strengthening practice

Make trivial decisions rapidly; take your time over serious ones.

Diversity

There were many unexpected occurrences for Don to deal with during the day, such as resolving disputes, responding to parents, caring for injured children and repairing equipment. The situation in primary schools where teachers are occupied almost continuously throughout the day means that there is a singular lack of 'slack' when unanticipated problems arise. Efficient teachers get into the habit of thinking ahead and trying to anticipate potential pressure points; however, unexpected incidents are, by their very nature, independent of the most careful planning. The introduction of PPA (preparation, planning and assessment) time offers teachers some respite from the face-to-face interaction but may do little to halt the overall sense of feeling 'driven'. To avoid becoming overwhelmed it is essential to pace yourself carefully, make lesson planning and teaching the priority and take on other responsibilities gradually.

Strengthening practice

You increase your chances of 'driving' rather than 'being driven' if you make good use of less busy times to alleviate likely pressure points in the day.

Fulfilment

The relational and affective ('things touching the emotions') dimensions of the job were highly significant for Don, and he gained great satisfaction from them. Don was encouraged and motivated when his lessons elicited a positive response from the children. Similarly, a pleasant or kindly word of appreciation from a parent lifted his spirits. Satisfaction and fulfilment in being a teacher emerge in a variety of ways but most notably through a belief that children have benefited and that 'significant others' – colleagues, assistants, parents – appreciate the work that they do. Teachers find fulfilment through the caring dimension of their role. Any attempt to reduce this element might reduce the intensity of teachers' work but at the same time deprive them of a major source of satisfaction. Caring is also reflected in formal parts of the curriculum, notably through the social and emotional aspects of learning (SEAL).

Strengthening practice

At the end of each day, write down three achievements and one thing from which you can learn.

Collegiality

Don was aware that as part of a team he owed it to his colleagues to keep abreast of the job and be supportive. A teacher's role in maintaining staff harmony and promoting collegiality is a key part of their identity but the busier they become the less time is available to provide support and encouragement for their colleagues. Trainee teachers become part of this company of people and their work is constantly open to scrutiny and evaluation, so it is best to view your colleagues and their advice as a helpful means of improving your overall competence as a teacher.

Terminology check

Collegiality describes a working situation in which there is mutual consideration and respect among colleagues and an absence of hierarchy.

Strengthening practice

Find out as quickly as you can what matters to the serving teachers and assistants and then show by your words and actions that those things matter to you as well.

Time management

The mismatch between the number of tasks that teachers have to complete and the time and energy available for them to do so inevitably results in a temptation to cut corners or neglect aspects of their work. However, partial commitment to the job results in diminished job satisfaction, guilt or subterfuge. Teachers are not machines and can only do their best but the most effective teachers are nearly always excellent time managers and target small pockets of time to achieve specific outcomes: for example, to check equipment, mark some work or complete a child's record.

Strengthening practice

Regularly ask yourself the question: 'Am I doing this task because it is necessary or because it is more enjoyable than other, more vital ones?'

Adaptability

Don manipulated some elements of the curriculum to fit his own priorities and agenda. In this regard, Troman and Woods (2000) refer to these subtle subversions of requirements as 'teacher adaptations', in which during times of intensity, teachers strictly limit the amount of innovation that they are willing to accommodate into their work cycle. However, Don was innovative by being strongly interactive in his teaching to draw out children's thoughts and ideas, using powerful visual images through technology, introducing practical work with a high degree of kinaesthetic learning ('learning by touching and doing') and strengthening the bonds with the class by reading amusing poems. He found this diverse approach personally satisfying as well as enlivening some of the more mundane parts of the day.

Strengthening practice

First, make sure that you have mastered the basics of lesson structure and teaching; then begin to adapt them using more imaginative approaches.

Impression management

Don was a conscientious and hard-working person but still needed to ensure that the significant people in his life recognised the fact. A world in which teachers are under increasingly close scrutiny means that creating the right impression is important for every practitioner. Naturally, trainees are in the business of demonstrating their competence to others and in this respect it is essential that you keep careful records of what you have achieved as evidence towards 'meeting the standards'; that is, towards meeting the requirements of the school placement. Avoid becoming obsessed with wondering what others think of you; at the same time be actively aware of the impression that you might be creating.

Strengthening practice

Form the habit of recording instances in which you achieved something of note, including the date of the event and, if possible, who witnessed the success – class teacher, teaching assistant, mentor or colleague.

Liaising with colleagues

Don did not always manage to liaise with other staff as successfully as he wished. Sometimes the non-availability of key personnel had a significant impact on the effectiveness of his work. Sometimes colleagues forgot things or were distracted by events that impinged upon their own working lives. Even in a school situation where collaboration and team-work are promoted, a large portion of the teacher's role involves a degree of detachment from colleagues due to the physical separation of classrooms, time pressures and the need to fit a lot of work into limited space. Although carving out opportunities to establish and maintain comradeship may prove hard in a busy day, it is a vital element of being a teacher.

Strengthening practice

Make as much effort to be personable with colleagues as you do with the children.

Role extension

A lot of Don's important work was carried out outside of the classroom door, including a combination of social contacts with parents, collaboration with colleagues, harnessing and managing resources, planning the curriculum, sorting out visits and special events, and liaising with teachers in other schools. While classroom teaching is the single most significant element of the role, it is by no means the only one. However, trainee teachers must, of necessity, focus their efforts on getting the teaching side of the job under control first and develop the other areas of the job as time and opportunity allows.

Strengthening practice

Whenever possible, use informal contacts with parents and colleagues to communicate about pupil progress, while being careful about privacy and sensitive issues.

Learning to cope as a teacher

Don's behaviour was influenced by expectations that he held of himself and that he perceived others held of him. *Learning to cope* was an additional and highly significant feature of the job on the occasions that he was under pressure during the day when he occupied several roles simultaneously. For instance, while in the playground he spoke to parents, managed groups of children, dealt with social conflicts, while mentally organising his teaching day. Don used a range of adaptive strategies to cope with the pressures induced by the constancy of these demands, including:

- the relegation of non-essentials to a minor position in the priority order
- delaying completion of less urgent jobs

- rearranging his schedule abruptly
- neglecting those tasks that could be left.

Don's role was therefore composite, less like a window composed of separate panes of glass than a multi-faceted diamond, each face sparkling or dimming during phases of the day. There were also a number of tensions in his role. Don was conscientious but forced to cut corners; hardworking but needing moments of respite; caring but succumbing to occasional brusqueness; a good time manager but finding that he was sometimes overtaken by events. Don employed a number of *practical* strategies to exercise control over the system, such as reducing the amount of energy he allocated to teaching subjects he did not enjoy, and *psychological* strategies of 'talking himself through' difficult situations as a means of composing himself and reaching a wise decision.

Strengthening practice

Write the words *Do it Now!* on card in large letters and place it somewhere prominent.

As an aspiring teacher it is important for two reasons that you are keenly aware of the factors influencing qualified teachers' daily work: first, because you are working with these teachers and need to recognise the demands on them; second, that before too long *you* will be that teacher. As a trainee, you should note the strategies used by teachers and assistants to protect their self-esteem, find pleasure in small achievements and preserve their physical and emotional strength. Don's message to you is that the job of teacher is one that offers enormous reward but can often be exhausting.

Extend your thinking

So, do you *still* want to be a primary teacher? Are you sure? Are you absolutely sure? Good for you!

Strengthening practice

Discuss with other trainee teachers the implications of the following:

- the different roles played by a primary teacher throughout the day
- strategies that teachers use to manage and cope with the many demands upon their time.

Professional learning perspectives

Challenges for new teachers

Research carried out by Jacklin *et al.* (2006) about the issues faced by new primary teachers indicated that one of the greatest challenges was taking full responsibility for the whole class, including establishing and enforcing boundaries of behaviour, pupil safety, registration, liaising with parents, and so on. Trainee teachers are partially protected from this all-encompassing role but still need to recognise that there is more to being a teacher than teaching lessons. The authors go on to say:

> Differentiated teaching, supporting and extending the least and most able pupils, and above all, setting high expectations and standards for all, irrespective of gender, ethnicity, race, disability or social background, are all part of the day to day role of a primary teacher. It is not surprising that beginning teachers can feel overwhelmed at times. (p. 78)

Emotional challenges for teachers

Day *et al.* (2007 pp. 243–4) in their study about teachers' lives, work and effectiveness conclude that teachers need to be able to manage successfully the cognitive [brain-power] and emotional challenges of working in different, sometimes difficult scenarios. The authors stress that managing the emotions attached to classroom life is fundamental to effective teaching and that investing energy in managing the emotional dimension is essential as each day teachers face pupils with varying degrees of learning needs, enthusiasm and desire for learning. Effective teachers will strive to engage with all of their pupils and this requires that they are able to bring reserves of emotional energy to their work. In other words, it is not only the children's welfare that should receive attention, but also that of the adults working with them. This principle has implications for the work-life balance of teachers and, of course, trainee teachers, who are subject to the same external influences as everyone else but have less direct control over what takes place in the classroom. The relationship between being contented and at ease outside school and your effectiveness inside school means that all practitioners must be careful to avoid working excessively long hours and being weighed down by petty issues; they also need to maintain strong supportive contacts with friends and family.

Find out more by reading

Liston, D.P. and Garrison, J.W. (2003) *Teaching, Learning and Loving*, London: Routledge.
Sedgwick, F. (2008) *So You Want to be a Teacher?* London: Sage.

The type of teacher you want to be

Points to consider as you read this chapter:

1   There is no single way to teach because each situation demands subtly different approaches.
2   Your progress as a teacher depends upon your own abilities, readiness to reflect thoughtfully on your classroom practice and willingness to learn from others.
3   Learning from others requires that you continually make careful, well-informed choices about suitable approaches to teaching and ways to behave as a teacher.

Factors influencing your development

We all have memories of our teachers, some of which leave us unmoved because although they contributed to our well-being and maturation, they made little specific impact on us as people. Other teachers will have made a powerful impression on our lives; their faces, voices and actions are etched into our minds, for better or for worse. Occasionally, a teacher will have had such an influence that she or he helped to turn our life around, give us fresh hope or spurred us to greater achievements than we ever thought possible. Such is the power and responsibility accorded to teachers.

What sort of teacher do you aspire to be? What do you want your pupils to say about you? How will you want to be remembered? What will be your epitaph? These questions are not trivial ones. They lie at the heart of success, for if you don't have a dream, how are you going to have a dream come true? As an aspiring teacher, you must try to avoid being carried along by pressures and forces that push you in a direction you do not wish to travel. You should hold tight to your aspirations, while recognising that you need to make adjustments to accommodate external demands, the school's priorities, the views of colleagues and parents, and your own evolving ideas, perspectives and professional knowledge.

As we saw in Chapter 2, teaching is a demanding and complex job and the many roles that a teacher occupies simultaneously require a combination of knowledge, skills, courage, perseverance and insight about human behaviour. The transition from 'student' to 'teacher' is never unproblematic and every trainee has to be prepared for a bumpy ride over some sections of the journey. It is not an easy task during a school placement to move from being an outsider to an insider; from being someone of no importance to someone of considerable importance; from being just another face to being *the* face. Trainees therefore rely heavily on more experienced teachers and tutors to guide and support them in their effort to become competent practitioners.

Terminology check

School experience and *school placement* are phrases used to describe a formally assessed period of time spent in school as part of a recognised course of training. *Teaching practice* is the old name for school experience and describes the time that you actively practise your teaching in front of children.

One of the things that you need to grasp from an early stage is that becoming a teacher is not like (say) learning to drive a train. Drivers have to learn to master the controls, recognise signals, maintain correct speeds over certain sections of the track and bring the train to a smooth halt. Train driving requires considerable skill but does not have to take particular account of the sorts of passengers on board or the countryside or the time of week, other than at a general 'safety and reliability' level. Whether the train travels from London to Brighton or from Cardiff to Aberdeen, the operational side is broadly similar. Over time, the driver learns to do the job well and becomes highly proficient – for which rail users are truly thankful. Teaching, on the other hand, while requiring the need to master basic skills of planning, organising, presenting the lesson and assessing pupils' work, has to take strict account of the *context* in which these operations are carried out. For instance, even within the same classroom, the presence or absence of a significant child, especially one who makes heavy demands upon adults, can change the dynamics markedly. The time of day, season of the year and state of the weather are also factors in the unique circumstances of a given situation on a specific occasion. For instance, anyone who has been in a primary school during a windy day will acknowledge the astonishing change in behaviour that such an apparently trivial factor can have on the children.

Terminology check

A *session* is an identifiable period of time spent on teaching and learning in a specified subject area.

A *lesson* is an identifiable unit of work that has to be fitted within a single or a multiple session.

Trainee teachers look forward to the day they become a qualified and competent teacher; the battles of the past will be over; they will be able to fulfil their dreams of working with children in an undisturbed environment; no more hassles; no more tears; no more emotional stresses and strains. Dream on! Teachers do not agree about everything but on certain points there is unanimity: the job is constantly evolving, children make unrelenting demands of you, and no two days are alike.

Extend your thinking

Many people claim that the most important thing in school is for teachers to make sure that children are learning. They are right … and wrong. Even when the lesson content and teaching is ordinary, children will still learn something. The most important thing is *what* children learn and how the *way* they learn affects their appetite for knowledge in the future.

Principles for mastering the job

While it is true that experience as a teacher allows you to learn the best ways of negotiating the day to day business and avoid making elementary mistakes in dealing with children and colleagues, it is nevertheless a fact that unlike the train driver mentioned earlier, you never fully master the intricacies of the job. Lists of standards, competences and other success criteria offer a structure for monitoring your progress as a teacher but achieving them to the satisfaction of your tutors and host teachers during school placement (see Chapters 8 and 9) should not be confused with the ability to operate as an effective teacher.

Success as a teacher relies solely on your ability to handle the *present* situation. Past competence is no certain guide to future success and counts for little unless you employ the knowledge and experience you have previously gained to influence what happens here and now. The necessity to carry forward the insights accrued from your hard-earned lessons and apply them to the immediate situation requires you to gain an understanding of the following:

- the way that children learn
- appropriate teaching methods
- the significance of your personality
- children's perspectives on learning
- the role of assessment in learning
- individual pupil needs
- utilising the skills of other adults
- communicating with pupils, colleagues and parents
- supporting colleagues, practically and emotionally.

All teachers have to master a broad range of skills, whether they are working with children who are barely five years of age or those about to go to secondary school: an ability to explain things clearly, command pupils' attention, organise and manage the lesson, collate and distribute resources, offer appropriate feedback, set targets for learning, liaise with colleagues, maintain records, and so forth. However, the way in which these skills are employed may differ sharply, depending on the age and abilities of the children. For instance, when teaching younger children it is normal to use a softer tone and speak at a steady rate, employ a larger range of colourful visual aids, divide a session into shorter sub-sections (as concentration spans of young children are generally briefer) and use repetition in learning through (for instance) chants, songs and rhymes. Younger pupils need time to play: both spontaneously with the equipment provided and 'adult-led' – where specific learning intentions are linked with the play situation. Older pupils usually respond to a more direct teaching approach, enjoy having teachers with a 'big' personality, revel in project work that continues over several days or weeks and are more competitive than they were as infants. They also need time to be playful, only unlike the younger children it is normally more closely organised by the teacher (e.g. in drama). Although it is not possible to be precise about the variations in teaching skills used with different ages of children, the need for flexibility in this regard is of paramount importance. As with many other aspects of the work, the best teachers never stop learning (see also Chapter 4).

Extend your thinking

'The one who dares to teach must never cease to learn'

(*Anon.*)

Finding fulfilment in teaching

People choose to teach for many reasons, not least the pleasure that they gain from being immersed in an environment in which a dedicated group of adults work alongside children with a united, though difficult to define, purpose called 'educating'. It is hardly surprising that teachers sometimes feel under the microscope in having to respond to so many different needs to satisfy the expectations of pupils, parents, colleagues, head teacher, governors, as well as the community and education inspectors. When things are going well, the approval from representatives of these groups is exhilarating; by contrast, their disapproval can bring distress and a loss of confidence.

Most of a teacher's fulfilment relies on establishing a secure, harmonious relationship with pupils; it is equally true that a critical comment from a significant person – such as a parent – can upset a teacher's sense of equilibrium and have a detrimental effect on his or her ability to teach and be innovative, as criticism usually evokes a 'play safe' approach. Doubts about personal competence can embed themselves in a teacher's mind, lower morale and constrain innovative practice. For this reason, peace of mind is not a cosy option for inadequate people but a vital necessity to ensure that teachers are operating at optimum efficiency and being daring rather than mundane practitioners. For trainees, the same sort of factors influence their states of mind, but the class teacher and tutor (rather than the head teacher, parents and inspectors) tend to be the touchstones for reassurance, as indicated by one trainee's comments:

> The teachers are very helpful, the tutors are very supportive and everybody seems to be really good, so that's made *me* feel really good and fairly confident.

In most jobs, after a stern word from the boss, employees make a more concerted effort to do better and 'move up a gear'; however, improving as a teacher is much more complex. Although there may be a small number of lazy and tardy individuals in school, the vast majority are highly diligent and determined to pour themselves out wholeheartedly for the job. Nothing less is expected from trainees, though inexperience sometimes means that their desire to be conscientious is frustrated by an incomplete understanding of how schools function and clumsiness with the 'nuts and bolts' of effective teaching and learning. To take a motoring analogy, experienced teachers know the route – having been that way many times before – and are highly sensitive to road conditions. They drive power-assisted vehicles with correctly inflated tyres, carefully adjusted wing mirrors and a satellite navigation system. They remain calm and are not fazed by unexpected events. By contrast, trainees tend to glue their eyes to the road ahead and rely considerably on physical signposts for guidance. Their vehicles have old-fashioned heavy steering, tyres are under-inflated and they are too preoccupied with basic manoeuvring to be over-concerned with the finer points of driving. They tend to be much slower in responding to unexpected situations and occasionally clip the kerb. After the first stage of the journey has been completed the experienced driver feels tired but soon recovers after a break and some sustenance. The inexperienced driver has used up a lot of nervous energy and feels too exhausted to eat or drink much. By the time they climb back into their respective vehicles, the two drivers are very differently prepared for the next stage of the journey. The experienced driver is refreshed and proceeds confidently; the inexperienced driver swallows hard, takes a deep breath and presses on, trying to appear more confident than he or she feels. Be reassured, however, that the transition from novice to expert is assisted by the fact that whereas the experienced teachers fly along the motorways, you will 'step up' from quiet country road to leafy suburban lane to main road before being let loose on the major highways of teaching. Bear in mind, too, that even the experienced practitioner still has things to learn, improve and master.

Taking responsibility in teaching

Some trainees are gripped with anxiety about the prospect of taking responsibility for a group of children – especially for a whole class – and with some justification. A considerable amount of skill, expertise and nerve is required in organising and managing 30 children, even with the support and assistance of other adults. It is common practice for trainees in the first few days or even weeks of the placement to supervise a group of children under the direction of the class teacher, gradually increasing responsibility until he or she is planning and teaching a full session. While you may be desperate to be trusted with the full class, the class teacher and mentor are aware of the mental and physical effort that constant teaching demands so ration your input. It takes time and experience to balance the effort expended with the psychological rewards from being in charge, as follows:

- Too little expenditure of effort + too little reward can lead to *despondency*.
- Too great expenditure of effort + too little reward will lead to *exhaustion*.
- Balance of expenditure and reward results in *satisfaction*.

The gap between arriving at the classroom door and assuming total responsibility for the whole class depends on numerous factors, including your previous experience and success in teaching a similar age group; the class teacher's disposition (some teachers are unwilling to 'let go' of the class; others cannot wait to do so); and the number of challenging pupils with which you will have to cope.

It may seem rather obvious to make the point that no two classes or two teachers are alike but it is a fact that needs to be taken into account by everyone concerned with assisting trainee teachers in school. Nowhere is this point better illustrated than in lesson planning and face-to-face contact with different

ages of children. Planning a lesson for younger pupils necessitates a keen awareness of many aspects of teaching and learning. Thus, reception and key stage 1
children will commonly:

- have a shorter concentration span than older ones
- be attracted by colourful visual aids
- prefer to 'do' rather than 'be told'
- find exciting stories fascinating
- enjoy funny events and people
- respond spontaneously and energetically
- act like mischievous puppies!

Older pupils also exhibit some of these traits but generally speaking, in comparison to younger children they are:

- passionate about their teachers (they love them, normally; or hate them,
  occasionally)
- able to assimilate a larger range of facts at one time
- capable of concentrating for longer periods of time
- enthralled by 'real life' examples (especially gory ones)
- inspired when they can see a purpose in what they are asked to do
- enthusiastic about practical and problem-solving tasks
- willing to offer an opinion and argue a point of view
- self-opinionated and occasionally cheeky.

Another key factor to consider is that nearly every class is a mixture of boys and
girls. Sometimes there is a preponderance of one sex or the other, which alters
the learning climate considerably: the minority group often struggles to assert
its presence; the majority group makes the heaviest demands. In general there
is a commonly held belief that boys underachieve in academic work and girls
excel themselves, whereas in fact, every group of children contains both high
and low achievers, and all stages in-between the extremes, so be cautious about
stereotyping. Myhill and Jones (2006) suggest that boys tend to believe that
their male teachers are more likely to have negative attitudes towards them but
to be condescending in their responses to girls. Boys believe that teachers value
girls more and like them better because of their good behaviour and willingness to hard work. They may well be correct.

The tendencies noted above should cause every trainee teacher to stop and
think carefully about the pupil 'audience', especially prior to, and at the com-
mencement of a new school placement. Teaching tips do not and cannot take
account of the children in your class: their age, maturity, attitude to learning and
intellect. For this reason, it always takes time to adjust to the circumstances of a
fresh situation and requires you to keep reviewing your decisions and adjusting
your lesson plans. It is also important to recognise that this professional learning

does not just happen; it necessitates a deep desire on your part to improve your own work as a teacher and help others to do the same.

Extend your thinking

Regardless of the pupil's age or sex, true learning is rooted in spontaneity, wonder and curiosity.

Your identity as a trainee teacher

As a trainee teacher you are in the 'interim world' between student and teacher. You are in charge of the children but not fully in charge. You are a member of staff, but only temporarily. You have to adjust to the school's priorities, which may be different from those of the previous school. You need to work very closely with a host teacher and tutor with whom you may or may not enjoy a comfortable relationship. In addition there might be a number of anxieties that commonly obstruct your progress, including concern about 'surviving' as a teacher, whether you have 'got what it takes' and if your supervisor's opinions about you are positive. Every trainee has misgivings from time to time, but you must try to combat them by using three techniques. First, remind yourself constantly that you are a capable person with the necessary qualities to teach; the host teachers were once in your position and you are no less competent than they were at your stage. Second, persevere and practise your teaching skills (see Chapter 7). Third, seek advice regularly; evaluate opinions; ask sensible questions; study to understand ways in which children learn best.

In seeking an identity for yourself as a teacher you need to step back and take a long hard look where your dreams are rooted to ensure that your aspirations take account of factors such as your own *personality* (things that come naturally to you, such as the ability to speak plainly; things that require diligent attention, such as handling criticism); your *intellectual capacity* (how easily and quickly you can absorb information; areas of learning you find difficult); and your *social skills* (relating to different people in a variety of contexts: one to one, small group, in a crowd, and so on). Listen to how some trainee teachers describe their favourite teachers. In doing so, notice the balance that each teacher achieved between being personable and caring, but also determined that the children would succeed academically and mature into well-rounded individuals. In turn the teachers were rewarded with the love and respect of the pupils:

> I enjoyed being a pupil in Mr Davies' class because he taught in a very fun and interesting way, which made me feel enthusiastic about his lessons and want to try hard. Although he was a fun teacher, pupils knew when to join

in and have a laugh but also knew that there was a boundary that should not be crossed that would make Mr Davies cross or annoyed. In many ways he was a feared teacher because nobody would ever take advantage of his humour by acting up; but this was mainly due to the respect that many pupils had for him.

Firstly, and most importantly, Miss Down was well liked. Of course, there is a fine line between being likeable and being a pushover, but she found the right balance because she was firm and tried to make learning fun. Another good quality of Miss Down's was her fairness. She treated all of her pupils the same and drummed into the class the importance of treating others how you would like to be treated. Her discipline system was the same for every child; there was no special treatment for those who usually behaved well and she never singled out children simply because they were usually the ones causing trouble. She gave every child the same chance and issued the same sanction for the same wrong behaviour, regardless of the child's history.

Mr Newman has been the teacher I most admired and respected. He always knew if there was a problem, either with the subject or outside of it. He was happy to talk things through and help us solve the thing that troubled us. I felt that I could go to him at any time when I needed assistance or reassurance about an issue. If one of us misbehaved, Mr Newman would look at the person and give a disappointed glance. If we didn't understand something, he would explain in a way that we could relate to by using examples from everyday life.

I was lucky enough to be taught by one of the best teachers I have ever come across. Mrs Woodbridge always had control of the class and knew how to make every child feel as if she was glad to have him or her in the group. She encouraged us to work through our problems together before coming to her and this helped us to take responsibility for our own learning. Although I always struggled with maths, Mrs Woodbridge made me believe that I could do it; she would explain things clearly and answer any questions I had, regardless of whether I thought they were stupid. She was always fair and would discipline children if they misbehaved, but she hardly ever needed to! Mrs Woodbridge showed us that she respected us, so we not only respected her, but also one another. She was a great teacher because she taught us important lessons about life, as well as formal work.

You may have noticed that all of the teachers had four characteristics in common:

1   The children respected them for their sincerity and commitment towards them.
2   They were unvaryingly enthusiastic and often had fun.

3   They stood no nonsense yet were approachable and responsive to individual needs.
4   They were concerned both with academic and social/emotional needs.

Although the extracts above offer only a glimpse of the teachers' personalities and characters, it is guaranteed that they were equally effective with parents and colleagues. In the next chapter we examine further the qualities and characteristics of an outstanding teacher.

> **Extend your thinking**
>
> What question would you like to ask each of the teachers mentioned in the extracts above?

Your vision for teaching and learning

If you were asked to describe your vision for teaching, I wonder what you would say. Perhaps you would use the sort of jargon so beloved of politicians about 'striving for excellence' or 'ensuring equal opportunity for every child'. You could employ populist phrases, such as 'teaching in a relevant and motivating way' or 'using creative approaches that inspire pupils'. Then again you might focus on aspects of children's learning and list aspirations for them such as 'reaching their potential' or 'achieving optimum achievement'. Hopefully, you would stress moral aspects such as knowing their place in the world and being a decent human being. In fact, a vision for teaching and learning comes in many and various guises; all of the aforementioned are relevant and, no doubt, you could easily add a number of others. Imagine, though, if your vision were couched in words like these: 'I want the children to do their best but most of all to be happy and good citizens' or 'I want to teach well but not to push myself so hard that my health and well-being suffer'. Visions do not *have* to be focused on achieving something exceptional.

The descriptions that follow offer formats through which a vision for teaching might be expressed. The summaries below are models – that is, they help to shape understanding rather than offering an exact description of what is real – and they provide an opportunity to compare and contrast the ways in which different philosophies about teaching and learning result in different approaches. What you believe to be important impacts upon the decisions you make about the job and the way you behave as a teacher. The four models can be identified using the following descriptors:

1   *Romantics*: when your imagination dominates the reality.
2   *Imitators*: when you try to copy another teacher.

3   *Chameleons*: when you are willing to freely change your approach.
4   *Entrepreneurs*: when you follow your instincts.

Romantics

Some trainee teachers are romantics and adopt a teacher role plucked from their imaginations. They believe that teachers stand at the front of the class and command instant obedience; teachers tell children what they need to know; teachers are invariably fair; teachers are respected and loved by the children, and so on. The problem with being fanciful is that it does not take account of the realities associated with the daily demands of classroom practice, liaising with colleagues, pleasing parents, meeting government targets and wider school involvement. As Maddock *et al.* (2007) warn, 'The demands on teachers' professional confidence are multiple: curriculum coverage, classroom organisation, pedagogical interactions [i.e. ways of teaching]; their confidence is not usually deployed in unlocking new doors, opening on to unknown spaces' (p. 50). The romantic teacher does not have to deal with fatigue, awkward children, filling in paperwork and coping with inspections. This imagined person is adored by everyone, floats in and out of the classroom like a dream and is undisturbed by circumstances. Romantic teachers never sweat, never despair and are never gripped by fear. Their working lives are seamless, punctuated only by joyful moments, laughter and celebration of achievement.

The advantage of having such a vivid imagination is that it energises and gives something to hold on to during the lean times. These aspirations are rooted in a 'somewhere over the rainbow' attitude to life; the future is bright and brimming with promise. In truth, it can be a great confidence booster to believe that tomorrow will bring unanticipated delight and a learning breakthrough for each child. We all need to have something of the romantic in our souls.

Extend your thinking

'Romance is the glamour that turns the dust of everyday life into a golden haze'

(*Anon.*)

Imitators

Some trainees tend to be *imitators*. They seize upon the attributes exhibited by teachers they admire and try to emulate them by adopting the same tone of voice, responses to children, use of rewards and sanctions, and even the way they relate to colleagues. The problem with being a clone of another teacher is that it can lead to unthinking forms of classroom practice and, in extreme cases, an inclination towards artificial behaviour; that is, copying a teacher's actions without considering the principles that underpin them. The trainee becomes an *imitator* (doing the same) but not a *ruminator* (considering why), so fails to interrogate the strategies that are being employed: Why is this approach best? How will this attitude enhance teamwork? What will be the result of acting in this way? Which methods are most likely to enthuse the children and shape learning? Unthinking trainees never progress beyond mediocrity because they lack the intellectual engagement to sharpen their practice. When people claim that such and such a teacher has not changed for years, they are wrong. Such a 'stick in the mud' teacher has actually been getting worse during that period of time.

The imitator role can, however, be beneficial if, at the same time, you undertake close observations of experienced teachers to discern the reasons underlying the strategies they employ in teaching and responding to the many situations they encounter each day. This thinking approach purposes to *reconfigure* the teacher's practice and adjust it to suit your personality and purposes. A view of imitation that serves to open your mind is highly beneficial if it extracts ideas from good practice rather than mindlessly replicating someone else's behaviour. A reconfigured form of imitation also tends to cement the bond between the trainee and the qualified teacher.

Extend your thinking

Imitation results in unimaginative practice; reconfiguration enhances and enlivens practice.

Chameleons

A small number of trainees resemble *chameleons* because they alter the way that they behave to blend in with the circumstances. If the host teacher is strict and demanding in (say) PE and relaxed in (say) Art, they track the mood closely. If the host teacher is warm and familiar with the children, the trainee acts in the same way, and so forth. If the children are noisy, the chameleon teacher gets louder and assertive; if the class are timid, the chameleon changes to being quiet and passive. While it is wise to be sensitive to the mood and disposition of the class, it is foolish to allow yourself to be a victim of circumstances in such a way that you behave randomly.

One problem with being a chameleon is that not every experienced teacher provides the inspiration and example that new teachers want to or should reflect in their work. A few teachers get disillusioned with the job; worn down by the constant demands and changing landscape of primary education. Some teachers are mediocre; they survive because they have learnt the short cuts and 'tricks of the trade'. They are adept at giving the right impression but would much rather be doing something different with their lives. Such teachers are poor role models and the dilemma for trainees is that if they are placed with them, they have to maintain a difficult balance between adjusting to the teacher's methods while maintaining their own preferred approach and integrity.

The advantage of chameleon blending, however, is that it encourages adaptability and avoids the onset of a kind of 'pedagogical paralysis' in following well-worn paths in predictable ways, while taking little account of the classroom context. Chameleons are great survivors in the wild as their changing camouflage helps them to avoid being eaten alive; trainee teachers sometimes feel as if they are faced with similar challenges in the classroom! They regard the chameleon option as a realistic way to cope with the demands of school experience, and who can blame them?

Entrepreneurs

Many people become teachers because they cherish the freedom to express their creativity, stimulate children by their enthusiasm and tap into spontaneous learning opportunities and pupils' interests. They want their classrooms to explode with colour, life and vitality. They long for children to explore and investigate; experiment, discuss and innovate. They highly value motivation.

The problem with being entrepreneurial is that school planning tends to leave little room for manoeuvre, especially if there are parallel classes or groups that need to remain broadly abreast of one another in working through the curriculum. Furthermore, your spirited attempts to offer a dynamic approach may clash with the host teacher's more methodical methods. Exploratory and enquiry-based learning do not always have fixed learning outcomes – the value is as much in the collaboration and thinking as in the result – which might be a concern if the trainee needs to demonstrate increasing pupil attainment.

The advantage of being an entrepreneur is that children normally respond positively to teachers who encourage them to find out by 'doing' and provide practical activities that allow them to explore and experiment. It is also undoubtedly the case that motivated children behave more responsibly than listless ones; occasional misdemeanours are usually caused by over-exuberance and not by wilful naughtiness. Innovative teaching flourishes if you adopt a perspective that views every child as possessing creative potential in an aspect of the curriculum, rather than seeing creativity as a quality that resides only in a small number of talented and gifted pupils.

Terminology check

Enquiry-based learning involves children finding out for themselves rather than being told by an adult.

Strengthening practice

To promote deeper learning use the following four strategies:

1　Incorporate spontaneous learning opportunities rather than allowing pre-determined learning objectives to become a straitjacket.
2　Encourage children to search for innovative solutions as well as predictable ones.
3　Extract the unusual from the usual by asking probing questions and speculating about possibilities.
4　Suggest and test hypotheses (tentative theories) and invite pupils to do the same.

Although you may have fond memories of that special teacher and opportunity to observe excellent classroom practice during your period of teacher training and education, it is never possible to replicate what you have seen, for the simple reason that you are not that teacher and you are teaching a different set of children. Even if you *were* teaching the same class, the children would behave differently with you from the way they do with the regular teacher. What you *can* do, however, is to give careful consideration to these talented teachers' attributes and decide how, in your own way, you can emulate them. Importantly, you should not merely observe what they do but consider the purpose that underpins their actions. In other words, don't just use your eyes; use your intellect.

Extend your thinking

In emulating a teacher it is essential to concentrate primarily on the thinking that underpins the behaviour, rather than simply copying the things that are said and done.

Professional learning perspectives

Complexity of the teacher role

Jeffreys (1971) stressed that although teachers should be *an* authority and *in* authority, they should not be authoritarian. A good teacher's authority stems from his or her knowledge, experience and wisdom, rather than from status or force of personality. In addition:

> Teachers need humour and humanity, sympathy and understanding. They must be able to tolerate trivial (though perhaps irritating) deviations, but

to stand firm on things that matter … One of the most valuable experiences for the young is to grow up in the company of older people who know their own minds, have clearly thought-out opinions, and cannot be influenced by fear or other emotional pressures. (p. 37)

Jeffreys also offered the following advice to teachers about adopting a proper attitude to the job, arguing that there is always a tension between teaching and learning. Thus:

The teacher can do no more than help one to learn. It is impossible to teach someone who will not learn … The pot has a right to argue with the potter. That does not mean that the teacher is superfluous, but only that the teacher's job is to help the plant to grow. That help is needed. It is impossible to learn without sources and means of learning, just as it is impossible to eat without food. (p. 57)

Committed and contented teachers

Much more recently, Sammons *et al.* (2007) conducted an extensive study of teachers' work and lives and their effects on pupils. One of the interesting conclusions that the team drew was that the more committed and resilient teachers were more likely to be effective in promoting pupils' academic outcomes. Thus: 'Attainments by pupils of teachers who are committed and resilient are likely to exceed those of teachers who are not' (p. 699). The authors argue that one of the most important factors in being successful and contented as a teacher lies in retaining enthusiasm and being well motivated, as much as engaging with curriculum-related issues, teaching approaches and defining the teacher's role.

Find out more by reading

Fay, J. and Fay, C. (2005) *Love and Logic Teacher-isms: Wise words for teachers*, Golden, Colorado: Love & Logic Press.
Holmes, E. (2005) *Teacher Well-being*, London: Routledge.

Chapter 4

A model of the ideal teacher

The content of Chapter 4 includes:

- a fictional case study to describe the ideal teacher
- key points from a case study to understand teachers as leaders
- strategies for fostering a positive learning climate.

Points to consider as you read this chapter:

1. How to achieve the attributes of an ideal teacher.
2. The sequence from being an onlooker to the pivotal figure in planning and teaching.
3. Ways in which teachers are able to promote a purposeful and productive learning environment.

Characteristics of an ideal teacher

What was your ideal teacher like? In what way was she or he ideal? Why does that teacher stand out in your memory so starkly? Let's explore the nature of the teacher's character and practice with reference to someone called Miss Palmer. First, we consider what was *untypical* of her.

Miss Palmer did not use a harsh or forbidding voice. She did not intimidate pupils by ordering them about, denying them time to respond after a command, staring grimly at them or threatening them with sanctions if they did not immediately comply. She did not wave away their attempts to express their opinions during a disagreement (however politely they offered them), nag them when they were in a mischievous mood (as all children are sometimes) or make no allowance for the different personalities of children in the class. Miss Palmer avoided using negative phrases, such as, 'What on earth are you doing, you silly child?' or 'I am sick of you lot!' or 'Jamie, stop your whinging'. She never showed her displeasure by ranting and raving, nor did she use sarcasm, injurious comments or threats.

So what characterised our lovely Miss Palmer? First and foremost, she was a *good communicator*. She looked children in the eye without being invasive and used animated facial expressions to denote delight and disappointment. Miss Palmer invariably spoke in a natural, unaffected tone and increased the intensity of her words rather than altering to a higher pitch when she wanted to stress a point. She did not hesitate to be insistent when it was necessary to do so (e.g. concerning health and safety issues) but generally preferred to cajole and beguile pupils, using a mixture of insistence and gentle flattery, accompanied by a pleasant but determined smile:

> 'Come on, Melanie. It's nice to see you thinking so hard but it will soon be Christmas!'

> 'Zophia, you've got such a happy face that I'd like to see it facing me, please, and not staring at Henry. Thank you.'

Miss Palmer possessed (or had developed) 'unforced energy' and a vitality that might have reminded an observer of a lava flow out of a volcano: cool on the surface but sizzling with power underneath; harmless in appearance but penetrating in its effectiveness. In part, this vibrancy was expressed by strong, direct and lively responses to children's comments and explanations. As well as listening carefully, she often added a comment of her own or asked a question or summarised what she thought had been said to her. If she misunderstood and was corrected by the child, she would throw her head back and laugh pleasantly: 'Oh, I see what you mean!' Other children would gather around or look up expectantly to savour the moment.

You will probably guess that Miss Palmer did not achieve such a high level of co-operation overnight. At the start of the year she was very firm and strongly (but not pompously) insistent. She was not moody but, on the rare occasions that she was a bit off-colour and temperamental, sufficiently gracious to apologise for her disposition when she had a 'bad day'. She smiled a lot but laughed less than she would subsequently do, and would not be drawn too far into informal conversations. Her comments were highly work-orientated and children gradually understood that if they wanted to tap into Miss Palmer's undoubted good nature, they would have to gain her trust and respect. This fact may puzzle you: 'Gain *her* trust and respect! Don't you mean the other way around?' Surprisingly, perhaps, the principle that pupils must earn the adult's respect is the way that every teacher should begin to develop an effective working relationship with children. You are the adult and teacher; they are the learners. You are the leader of the class; they follow your example and direction. You are learning, too, of course, but as far as the children are concerned, your role is to liberate them to discover the wonders of the unknown: they have to decide how they respond to such overtures.

Extend your thinking

You cannot force pupils to learn. They will learn when motivated to do so. The process is a combined operation, you and the children working in tandem.

Classroom leadership

In understanding the leader–follower relationship, it is important to realise that children are, in some ways, like *disciples*, in the sense that they accept your superior knowledge, experience, wisdom and understanding, and look to you to provide moral authority, teaching and direction. You, in turn, offer clarity of purpose, encouragement and reassurance. However, children are also like *fellow travellers*, in as much as the learning 'journey' unfolds for both adult and child alike. Pupils are not, of course, passive recipients of information, but rather like sponges that are most absorbent when they are already moist. A dry sponge is far less effective than a damp one for the simple reason that the movement of moisture relies on the suppleness (or 'sponginess') of the material and cannot travel easily through hard and stiff fibres. In the same way, if you succeed in whetting children's interest by your enthusiasm, sparkle and ability to make work a joy rather than a grind, they are much more absorbent ('damp') and likely to relish learning and tolerate the less appetising portions.

Good classroom leaders like Miss Palmer also recognise that an important element of their leadership is to draw on the existing knowledge, spontaneity and eagerness residing in the body of pupils that comprises the class. As Dalton and Fairchild (2004) argue:

> Some of your best teaching flows spontaneously from your deepest intuition. At its core, teaching is the artistry of creating experiences that lead people into greater awareness. It's an artistry of knowing the moods, needs and expectations of your pupils, while staying fully aware of your own. (p. viii)

Children, especially young ones, may have a limited grasp and experience of life, but the sum of each small contribution results in a pool of knowledge fragments and flickers of insight that good teachers affirm and nurture. For instance, the child of a garage mechanic might possess an understanding of car engines that would surpass that of most teachers. A child from an immigrant family will probably speak two or more languages and offer a different cultural perspective on familiar situations. The child of a computer programmer will almost certainly be more at home with technology than many adults. It would be an appalling waste of human resources to ignore the hidden treasures of capability and expertise that lies untapped behind every child's visage. Miss Palmer was far wiser than to overlook such heaven-sent opportunities.

> **Extend your thinking**
>
> One of your roles is that of shepherd. Some shepherds drive the flock from the rear; others lead the flock from the front. Both types of shepherd are leaders of a sort, but those at the rear tend to coerce the sheep, while they follow those at the front willingly. Which type of shepherd would you like to be: a coercer or a coaxer or a mixture of the two types?

Miss Palmer's seductive powers of persuasion and the way that she was able to steer children along the right path, yet take account of their feelings and preferences, allowed her to appear as if she achieved compliance effortlessly. In fact, like the well-known analogy of the swan gliding across the water, she worked hard to ensure that she succeeded and did not rest on her laurels. She was also the undisputed leader of the pack.

Summary of Miss Palmer's approach

It was invariably true that she:

- communicated directly and assertively with pupils
- spoke clearly, firmly and politely
- achieved obedience without damaging pupils' self-esteem
- was respectful towards children even when annoyed with them
- drew on previously considered strategies when reacting to situations
- maintained eye contact with children without being invasive
- separated the person of the child from the behaviour
- expected to be obeyed (and nearly always was)
- quickly restored a working relationship with a pupil after a tense encounter
- encouraged children to offer their viewpoints
- promoted group interaction and sharing of ideas
- always found a positive dimension in every situation.

Summary of things she did not do

She did not ...

- try to intimidate children
- nag and harangue children for misdemeanours
- hesitate to deal with disruption
- hesitate to admonish a child when necessary
- get angry and strained under difficult circumstances
- feel guilty about her failings and lapses

- blame children for her shortcomings
- view disruption as a sign of failure
- allow individual pupils to dictate patterns of classroom interaction
- hope that good discipline would result from kind words
- use hurtful comments
- search for things to complain about.

The Miss Palmers of this world are not perfect teachers. They have their good and not-so-good days. They have moments of despair and peaks of exhilaration. Some of their lessons are exceptional: children are highly motivated, keen to learn, deeply embedded in the tasks and activities, enjoying every moment. The majority of their lessons are acceptably good: children listen politely with moderate levels of enthusiasm; the tasks are completed efficiently and the end of the lesson concludes pleasantly. A small number of lessons are disappointing: children are restless, learning is superficial and the end of the session is a welcome relief. If you want to emulate or exceed Miss Palmer's achievements, you must be willing to persevere, get advice from anyone who is willing to give it to you, rehearse and hone your teaching skills until they become second nature, learn about the process of learning, study to improve your subject knowledge, prioritise your time, relate to parents, find ways to get paperwork jobs completed and offer wholehearted support to colleagues. You won't have time to get bored, that's for sure.

Extend your thinking

The factors that determine whether or not a lesson will be excellent, mediocre or poor depend on two principal factors: the children's attitude to learning and your attitude as you teach them.

Fostering a positive learning climate

I hope that you have caught a flavour of the qualities exhibited by memorable teachers like Miss Palmer and it has helped you to think more carefully about the sort of teacher you want to be. The best trainees are commended for their rapport with the class, decisiveness, sense of humour and determination. They insist on the highest standards but are sympathetic towards children who struggle. Top quality trainees soon become a welcome addition to the staffroom and there is sincere disappointment when they finish the placement (see Chapters 8 and 9). There are well-established strategies and techniques to promote a productive learning climate and the following factors offer a summary of the key ingredients, which taken together offer you a good chance of achieving your ambition of fostering a positive working environment.

Be welcoming

Make every effort to show pupils that you are pleased to see them and glad to have them there, using 'soft' eye contact and making encouraging comments. Chaplain (2003) suggests that eyes transmit two types of information. First, they indicate that you are prepared to receive information by showing that the lines of communication are open. Second, they demonstrate your interest in the other person or persons. In practice you may want to position yourself by the door and welcome children as they arrive. Close physical proximity and (in the case of younger children) a willingness to put your head at the same level as theirs, also acts to enhance the quality of communication by blurring the formal adult–child boundaries, while maintaining the core of your relationship. The concept of 'blurring the formal boundaries' means that you ease your privileged adult status; 'maintaining the core' means that despite the blurring you retain the right at any given moment to revert to a formal relationship if a child tries to take advantage of your gracious approach. Some trainees are nervous about being friendly with pupils for fear of 'losing control'; however, if you maintain the core by insisting on courtesy and reasonable behaviour, it minimises the chances of any unwanted consequences. One way or another you must persevere to show children that you really do enjoy their company and they can, if they behave appropriately, enjoy yours.

Extend your thinking

Consider the adverse effect on your relationship with the children if they get the impression that you are happier to see them go than to arrive.

Be scrupulously fair

The most frequently muttered expression issuing from disgruntled children is: *It isn't fair!* Although you cannot hope to, and should not try to pacify children, it is important that you explain why decisions have been taken, console those who don't quite make the grade despite earnest endeavour and hold out the promise of further opportunities for pupils not chosen. However, in attempting to be fair-minded, it is important not to give children the impression that you have something for which to apologise – unless, of course, you have made a genuine error. Additionally, a small percentage of children use the excuse that life treats them unfairly as a tactic to avoid confronting their limitations and failures. A sulky pupil, who regularly complains that he or she is hard done by, and may even persuade a parent to come in to school or write to complain, is probably unhappy and insecure. Children prosper when they know that adults like them, but it is a fact of life that you won't like all children equally well. Nevertheless, your attitude must be constructive towards each pupil, seeking to find ways to approve his or her behaviour, as well as commending the work they produce. It is nearly always true that the best-loved teachers make a regular effort to find something endearing in every child and invariably succeed in doing so.

Extend your thinking

It is important to try to respond to your pupils unconditionally. That is to say, to treat the children who irritate and challenge you with the same courtesy and concern as the children you like and admire.

Be consistent

All teachers have miserable days when they speak and respond in an uncharacteristically abrupt or grumpy fashion, but do your best to ensure that your approach is steady, unflappable, relaxed and alert. If children become wary about approaching you it reduces the quality of communication and, in the case of timid pupils, may cause them considerable anxiety. Consistency does *not* mean that you 'treat all children the same' but rather that you model qualities such as helpfulness, a willingness to listen and explain, and a non-discriminatory attitude on the basis of factors like gender, background, race, physical prowess or attractiveness. If you are going to be consistent, be consistently good, of course, not consistently poor.

Extend your thinking

Consistency must not be confused with 'sameness'.

Be cheerful

Some trainee teachers think that by looking grim and a bit fierce they will somehow come across as being professional and sophisticated. In fact, an unsmiling demeanour is usually interpreted as moodiness or negativity, which is usually reflected in similar responses from pupils and colleagues. A pleasant expression and bright manner has the opposite effect. Smiling at children is not a sign of weakness; it is a necessary form of social contact in much the same way as a handshake or a salute in the military. Even when a stern warning or rebuke is necessary, there is little to be gained by being unpleasant if, in doing so, you destroy the bond between you and the child. The only exception is when a child has been unkind or bullied another pupil, in which case sternness is required. Finding a balance between firmness and congeniality is not easily struck but can usually be done without sounding miserable.

Terminology check

Sternness is being strict and uncompromising but respectful towards the person.

Assertiveness is courteously but confidently stating your opinion or belief without offending others.

Nastiness is being spiteful and malicious towards someone.

Be organised

It is almost impossible to be an effective teacher – and certainly an effective trainee teacher – without being well organised at every level. Basically, you have to be a straight thinker: What am I doing? Why am I doing it? What is the best way to achieve it? Being well organised should not be confused with a clinical, 'correct' approach that is *efficient* but not particularly *effective*. The classroom appearance also plays an important part in learning, so spend a little time each day ensuring that the room is orderly, with everything in its place, properly labelled and correctly positioned. Even if the room is a little untidy it should be functional. The best-organised teachers *first* have to sort out themselves. Disorientated, muddled teachers usually create messy, disorganised pupils; the opposite is also true. Imagine that there is an invisible stranger who observes you at work inside and outside school. What grades would the mysterious observer give you for your organisational qualities?

Strengthening practice

Make *a proper place for everything* one of your class mottos.

Terminology check

Efficiency is the ability to do something well or to achieve a desired result to the minimum level necessary, without wasting energy or effort.

Effectiveness is also bringing about the desired or intended result, while creating an appetite for learning and fostering enthusiasm for extending the boundaries of knowledge.

Be keen to learn

Host teachers on school placement place a lot of emphasis on a trainee teacher's level of receptiveness to advice, readiness to volunteer for jobs, sensitivity to the feelings of colleagues and general willingness to work as a junior member of the team. It may be difficult to view yourself as a colleague rather than as a student, but it is essential to make the effort to do so. When listening to a tutor or teacher offer advice or explain a situation, it is a useful strategy to say something to the effect: 'Thank you, I had not thought of that idea' or 'I must write down that suggestion before I forget it' or 'I will go and do that now while I think about it'. One way and another it pays to show that you are keen to learn and also to contribute. It may also surprise you to know that many teachers feel quite insecure and are glad to have someone like you around to assist, support and to offer unobtrusively a different perspective on their role. In doing so, ensure that you don't give the impression that the teacher would improve if only she followed *your* advice!

Extend your thinking

Responding positively to advice from the host teachers signals the fact that you want to be part of the team.

Be courteous

There is a myth that circulates among some inexperienced trainee teachers that children respect them more if they raise their voice and suppress poor behaviour by dint of their forceful personality. In fact, the best teachers are invariably polite with pupils and deal with infringements by being grave rather than exploding in a fit of angst. Courtesy towards children should not, however, be confused with feebleness. Children despise adults who come across as emotionally inadequate and hesitant about being decisive. Your colleagues, too, will expect to be treated with civility. A pleasant comment, cheerful remark and hearty laugh (at the appropriate time) will transform the atmosphere and other adults will see you for the person you are and treat you accordingly. It goes without saying that 'wisecracks' and snide comments are strictly off bounds. Be charming but remember that teachers are being paid to do a job and will not have the luxury of 'escaping' back to college after a period of time, so avoid jesting about serious issues.

Extend your thinking

Are people laughing with you or, secretly, *at* you?

Be modest

One of the most winsome characteristics of exceptional people is their modesty. They don't need to show off, brag about their exploits, successes or achievements. In fact, they seem genuinely surprised when other people congratulate them on how well they have done. You should aim to develop such an attitude of mind by looking away from yourself and concentrating on the welfare of others. This attitude is not a clever piece of reverse psychology to fool people into admiring you; it is an attempt to allow your qualities to rise naturally to the surface, rather than publicising them. Of course, it is important to use the talents and abilities you possess to the full and not hide them away as if they were something shameful; yet you have to avoid giving the impression that they make you superior. You may be brilliant when it comes to PE, but can you teach music? You may be outstanding when handling the whole class during interactive maths, but can you help children with advanced reading skills? Teachers cannot be exceptional in every area but it is better to be a good all-rounder than it is to be wonderful in a few areas and poor at everything else. If you are besotted with a single subject, try teaching secondary aged pupils instead.

Extend your thinking

'You aspire to great things? Begin with little ones'

(*Saint Augustine*)

'The first shall be last and the last, first'

(*Jesus Christ*)

Be personable

There is a difference between being *personable* (likeable and charming) and *personal* (intimate) in your exchanges with pupils. Children love to tell the adults they trust about key events and moments from their private lives, especially if the adult responds enthusiastically. Children are also fascinated by teachers' private lives, particularly their sporting and musical achievements, and are delighted if a teacher shares something of their interests and (perhaps) family situations with them. On the whole it is better to be cautious about sharing too much in the early stages of meeting a new class or group. Once you have established yourself as a teacher you can use snippets of information about your life outside school to enhance your reputation, stimulate curiosity and foster intimacy. However, beware of talking about your own situation too freely, too often, or you may be perceived as naïve by staff and considered a bore by pupils. If children ask you for your opinion about a controversial or sensitive subject, it is best to lay out the options first: 'Some people believe (this) and some people believe (that) but I believe ...' or say that you are still weighing things up. Always follow up by asking the child who has requested your opinion what he or she thinks. Do not dismiss a child's odd-sounding viewpoint; the child may be reluctant to offer one again and it probably reflects what the child's parents believe. If the pupil makes a sneering comment, you should explain calmly why that attitude is unhelpful and discuss the matter confidentially with the class teacher as soon as possible.

Extend your thinking

There are times to give a straight answer and times when is it appropriate to say, 'That is private'.

Be amazed

Some teachers expect that pupils will be enthralled by the work but fail to exhibit any passion themselves. They are then disappointed that their teaching is having so little impact and may complain to pupils about their poor attitude. However, if you show a sense of curiosity, inquisitiveness and wonderment, the children will quickly be drawn into the learning and gradually develop similar traits. Your 'astonished' attitude will also inexorably draw you towards a more problem-solving pedagogy, rather than a bland 'find the answer' approach. Curiosity is best satisfied when learning is presented in the form of issues to be resolved, as well as facts to be stored, so use of a range of 'open' and 'speculative' questions is essential in opening up children's eyes and minds to other possibilities. Your amazement should also be evident when children tell you something about their lives (such as a visit to a friend's house) or show you a precious photograph (of a visit to a theme park, for instance) or a possession (e.g. a birthday present). In this regard, you must learn to be childlike (as opposed to childish) and see life from their point of view.

Extend your thinking

'I have no special talents. I am only passionately curious'

(*Einstein*)

Be playful

All children and many adults love to play. It releases tension, excites interest and stimulates ideas. Being 'playful' is a related but different concept. Playfulness requires a willingness to take a gently 'sideways' look at life, to keep events in proportion and be willing to engage with the softer side of a child or colleague's personality. Humour has an important part to play in oiling the wheels of learning and is different from merely being funny or 'playing to the gallery' in a vain attempt to remedy other problems by recourse to an immature and embarrassing jokiness. Being playful allows you to see the lighter side of situations, to be serious but not grim, to be dedicated without becoming obsessed, and to aim high while ensuring that there is a comfortable landing when things go wrong. Most 'playful' adults are described by children as 'good fun' or similar but beneath the good humour is deeply rooted determination and professionalism. The teacher who can both 'dance and sing' as well as provide much-needed expertise and knowledge is every pupil's and parent's dream.

Extend your thinking

'It is a requisite for the relaxation of the mind that we make use, from time to time, of playful deeds and jokes'

(*Thomas Aquinas*)

Be fascinating

We all like interesting people and children are no different in this regard. A fascinating person elicits curiosity, encourages questions, stirs the imagination and provides a fresh perspective on familiar events. Most trainees are energetic characters outside school, brimming with personality and ideas; but some of them seem to leave their characters behind them at the classroom door and lapse into a reserved and rather uninspiring disposition. Make sure that you don't make the same mistake. Most successful teachers carry an air of mystery, which they transmit through quiet smiles, effective use of the eyes and the ability to cause even the most sceptical child to say 'wow!' Being fascinating is not, of course, the same as being (as the children might say) a bit weird. While tales about your 'around the world' backpacking trip will probably amaze and excite, a silver trophy for ballroom dancing might not have quite the same impact! Nevertheless, it is good to let pupils know about your own achievements and experiences, especially if they are in the area of sport, music or stage. Just as you enjoy celebrating children's achievements, so they love to take a pride in their teacher's exploits.

Extend your thinking

It is preferable to be your pupils' hero than to be an irrelevance.

Be encouraging

Some teachers are naturally encouraging; others seem reluctant to offer positive comments unconditionally. It pays to distinguish between *encouragement* (which can and should be constant) and *praise* (which should be used more sparingly).

Tauber (2007) offers a useful analysis of the different characteristics attached to encouragement and praise. He suggests that whereas praise is a reward given by an adult for completed achievement, encouragement is an acknowledgement of the *effort* made by a child. Praise implies that pupils have fulfilled the adult's expectations, while encouragement helps children to evaluate their own performance and achievements. Encouragement boost pupils' esteem, promotes respect and acceptance, and is given without conditions. This final point (encouragement given without conditions) is important because it is common to hear a teacher encouraging or praising a child in one breath, only to point out shortcomings in the next. There is, of course, a place and time to offer feedback and guidance to children (referred to as formative assessment or 'assessment for learning', AFL) but it is worth trying to separate the encouraging types of comments that are used to celebrate achievement from the developmental ones that are used in the process.

Terminology check

Encouragement: acknowledging the child's effort.

Praise: acknowledging the result of the child's effort.

Be firm

Every trainee teacher wants to be liked by the children, but if this desire becomes obsessive it can detract from being decisive, clear and insistent and leads to 'fishing' around with words to test the children's reactions, rather than saying what needs to be said to maintain classroom order and telling pupils precisely what you want them to do. Surveys to determine what type of teacher is most popular nearly always place those with firm but fair approaches near the top. The reason for this rather surprising pupil attitude is simple: children like to know where they stand and who is in charge. They will have little time for you if they perceive that you are unreasonable or nasty or distant, but your confident 'no nonsense' manner, streaked with humour and a sense of proportion about childish misdemeanours, provides the secure learning climate in which they feel free to explore ideas, express opinions and strive for excellence. When the children go home at night and tell their parents and friends about events during the school day, they invariably refer to their teacher's actions. If you have dealt with a situation firmly, your reputation is enhanced and parents get to know that you are a decisive person in whom they can have confidence; if you allow pupils to 'get away' with inappropriate behaviour, the opposite happens. Being firm helps to facilitate a positive and orderly working environment. See Chapter 6 for further details.

> **Extend your thinking**
>
> What sort of reputation do you want to have with (a) children, (b) colleagues, (c) parents?

Be lively

Learning should be enjoyable most of the time and engaging pupils for all of the time. If it is not, the children will soon let you know by their listless attitude, restlessness and, perhaps, expressing their grievance in a variety of undesirable ways, such as yawning loudly, fiddling with their clothes, mouthing words to friends, making silly sounds, staring out of the window, doodling or lolling about. It is not possible to make every lesson 'sing and dance' but by trying to inject a sense of adventure into sessions, explaining the relevance and importance of less-than-thrilling content and maintaining a cheerful demeanour, you increase the likelihood that pupils will co-operate and respond positively. It is also beneficial if you strive to help children extend their learning beyond the immediate, predetermined learning outcome by pointing out the links with other curriculum areas. In short, you are more likely to keep the children on board by speaking and acting in a lively fashion than if you adopt a grimly determined approach. If the children are reluctant to finish their tasks or raise numerous trivial issues about the activity or get silly, you can be reasonably certain that pupils are interpreting your liveliness as artificial, so strive to be genuine.

> **Extend your thinking**
>
> Teachers can be 'lively' from the moment they enter the room and before they speak a word as they communicate through their body language. However, liveliness cannot cloak inadequacy of preparation or a failure to establish a strong bond with pupils.

Be compassionate

Aim to be compassionate but not sentimental. Children (and most adults) know instinctively if you are being kind because you think it is in *your* best interest to behave that way or because you think it is in *their* best interest to do so. Compassion extends beyond the classroom walls into the corridors, playground and staff room, reflecting a willingness to face up to the realities of life and put others first. It exceeds mere pity and is demonstrated by a willingness to sympathise and to offer consolation and practical advice about solutions. Sometimes the best form of compassion is simply to listen and to try to understand what the person is saying; on such occasions, silence is golden. O'Quinn and Garrison (2004) go so far as to argue that it is essential to create *loving relations* in the classroom. Thus:

> Empathy, compassion, commitment, patience, spontaneity and an ability to listen are all closely connected to the trust necessary for creating the conditions for loving relations in the classroom community. (p. 63)

Be thorough

Whether you are planning, organising resources, teaching or assessing children's work, the key word is 'thoroughness'. Thus, planning should take account of all the ingredients necessary for an efficient session; resources should be appropriate for the task and readily available; teaching approach should be wholehearted; and assessment should be sensitively conducted. In particular, your active engagement with the children must be of high quality by picking up on important points, offering well-judged comments and reinforcing children's understanding and knowledge development. Avoid the dreary practice of lessons in which there is a 'warm-up' phase that has nothing to do with the main lesson; a question-and-answer session that is little more than allowing the more able children to repeat what they already know; a task phase that is introduced rapidly and concluded prematurely; and a plenary (summarising time) that consists of nothing more than heartily congratulating a small selection of children while the majority look on as spectators. It is better to target less subject content in a lesson but to do so comprehensively, than to supposedly 'cover' more content but to do so superficially. Kelly (2005) suggests that children learn better if they are seen as 'craft apprentices' rather than 'unskilled labourers' and warns against the 'production line' mentality in which the teacher 'controls the transmission of ready-made packages of knowledge by providing appropriate tasks and then monitors and assesses their acquisition' (p. 67). By adopting such an unimaginative approach, children's learning is almost completely motivated by a desire to complete the work and do well in tests. By contrast, you are more likely to create the conditions for deep learning by involving children as junior co-participants in learning, teaching them necessary skills, promoting their thinking, exploring ideas and allowing them to investigate themes, rather than piling on task after task in a vain hope that some knowledge and understanding 'sticks' in their minds.

Terminology check

Apprentices learn from the master craftsman by observing, listening to advice, imitating, thinking and developing their own distinctive expertise.

Labourers just do as they are told.

Be courageous

Courage may not instantly come to mind when considering the role of teacher but it is, in fact, an essential quality to possess. Teacher courage is different from the bravery displayed (for instance) by soldiers in battle, a lifeboat crew or an astronaut, where a specific task has to be accomplished at great personal cost. Teacher courage requires that you develop a 'stickability' to persevere when children are restless, face up squarely to your own shortcomings, refuse to compromise your core beliefs and show a willingness to deviate from your plans to accommodate pupil interest despite pressure to conform. These qualities are not easily acquired. It is far simpler to resort to blaming or scolding children rather than to scrutinise your own practice or gain necessary advice that may be rather unpalatable. It is easier to discard your attempts to develop a positive classroom climate by resorting to hectoring, giving 'heads down' tasks and initiative-stifling sanctions than to hone your skills as a mediator and encourager. It is also easier to teach didactically (directly) than to provide opportunities for pupils to collaborate, explore and solve problems, with higher risks of task deviation and unanticipated outcomes attached to them. Courage should not, of course, be confused with foolhardiness. As a guest in the school you have to learn to orientate in the direction of the predominant teaching approach and respect existing practices. Be a warrior, not a worrier!

> **Extend your thinking**
>
> 'Don't follow where your path may lead. Instead, make your own way and leave a trail'
>
> (*Anon.*)

Be eager

Everyone loves to see a new teacher working hard and 'getting stuck in', but it is not only the capacity to be busy that matters but to be busy doing things of significance. While you should never be reluctant to lend a hand with basic tasks, there is a danger of becoming trapped in a cycle of activity that drains your energy but contributes little to your development or pupil learning. Eagerness is not a quality that can be turned on at will; it is driven by confidence and high motivation level. Sometimes the new situation is daunting and you may initially struggle to be enthusiastic. It is also possible to be *so* eager that you irritate the host teacher by your incessant questioning, artificial smiles and contrived laughter. Eagerness is best expressed by 'being there' for the teacher, quietly and calmly going about your business and maintaining an open channel of communication with colleagues. There is, of course, no place for trainees with ostentatious and obtrusive personalities, who think schools exist only for their benefit. It creates a good impression if you volunteer to do something; it creates an even better one if you get on and do it without being asked. Nevertheless, it pays to weigh up the situation before launching into a major commitment that may, in a short space of time, lose its attractiveness and become a chore.

Extend your thinking

'A volunteer is worth twenty pressed men'

(*Old proverb*)

Be inclusive

It is an accepted principle that every child deserves a fair chance, should be treated with appropriate kindness and consistency and enabled to learn well, be happy and satisfy his or her aspirations. As a teacher you will need to ensure that each child is given suitable learning challenges and that you respond to their diverse learning needs. All children have to overcome potential barriers to learning, including conceptual (ability to grasp knowledge) and language limitations. Pupils for whom English is not a first language ('English as an additional language', EAL) may learn to speak and write but not possess the cultural insights that make learning meaningful (see Gregory, 2008). Some children who struggle with English (including language impoverished indigenous pupils for whom English is the first language) may excel in an area that does not depend as heavily on the written or spoken word, such as arithmetic, drama or physical activity. Other children are not used to listening or simply cannot absorb what an adult says because of communication difficulties (see Chapter 5). Sometimes these problems are severe and require intervention programmes involving, perhaps, an adult assistant or (in the most extreme case) an external specialist teacher. There is no doubt that children's home backgrounds also markedly affect their ability to learn: some new school entrants may have been discouraged from asking questions and received little stimulation other than from being immersed in television programmes and electronic games. Others will have experienced a rich diet of positive reinforcement and encouragement from adults, and situations that facilitate language acquisition and foster initiative. Catering for this wide range of abilities and accommodating children from different backgrounds is one of the major challenges for you as a teacher. It is no exaggeration to say that it is in this area that the battle is lost or won.

Every Child Matters

Every Child Matters: Change for Children (commonly referred to by the acronym, ECM) is a Government initiative that seeks to protect and improve the well-being of children and young people from birth to age 19, so that all children, whatever their background or their circumstances, have the support they need to:

- be healthy
- stay safe
- enjoy and achieve
- make a positive contribution
- achieve economic well-being.

In practice, it involves closer liaison between all agencies that provide services to children, including voluntary groups, the police, social services, child protection groups and (even) hospitals. The ECM initiative also seeks to help children and young people fulfil their aspirations, hopes and dreams. In effect, *Every Child Matters* is a way of formalising what every sincere primary teacher already does, namely, to put the welfare of the 'complete' child – body, mind and spirit – at the heart of the educative endeavour. Church schools have been encouraged to define, evaluate, develop, express and celebrate their distinctive Christian approach to the implementation of ECM, encapsulated in the expression 'every child matters to God'. That is, adults working with children in any capacity should have a concern for their total well-being, based on the premise that each child is accepted and respected as unique and precious to God.

Under the 2004 Children Act, schools are required to respond to the Every Child Matters Agenda, including *combating bullying*. Anti-bullying strategy normally makes particular reference to the need for children to be physically, mentally and emotionally healthy and safe from victimisation and discrimination. Teachers therefore need to encourage the development of positive relationships, positive behaviour and choosing not to bully others by:

- providing information relevant and appropriate to the age and developmental stage of the pupils
- helping pupils to develop skills of assertiveness, communication and effective dialogue in relationships, including anger management
- encouraging the exploration and clarification of values and attitudes, rights and responsibilities
- fostering self-esteem, positive self-image and confidence.

Curriculum topics to achieve the above aims include areas such as:

- feelings and relationships
- personal safety
- lifestyles and culture
- growing up
- conflict resolution
- coping with peer pressure.

School can be quite a daunting place for some children, especially if they have experienced failure or been on the receiving end of criticism from adults or disparaging remarks from their peers. It does not take long after a child's tentative answers to questions have been met with sighs from the teacher and quiet sniggers from around the group for that child to retreat into the safety of anonymity. It is essential that you capture hearts and minds by extolling and modelling a keen awareness of children's feelings and sincerely acknowledging publicly their courage in offering a comment or attempting something difficult. Most children are contented and cheerful, but a few are weighed down by concerns about school, home or friendships. You can make a significant difference to the life of a child by being friendly and offering strategies and supportive advice to ensure that the child copes and succeeds. Compassion is sending out a message to adults and children alike that you have a sincere interest in their welfare. It can be cultivated by making a determined effort to see caring and nurturing as an essential part of your role.

Extend your thinking

'Every Child Matters' is not just the title of a Government initiative; it's an attitude of mind every teacher should embrace.

Professional learning perspectives

Teachers as models

In 1987 Rachel Pinder published a book with the provocative title, *Why don't teachers teach like they used to?* in which she emphasised the importance of the teacher in being a 'model' for children and an example to colleagues and parents. Thus:

> Clearly, the way teachers speak to their children, their manner towards them, as well as the content of their speech is all influential. If we want the children whom we teach to be thoughtful, we must be thoughtful towards them; it is we who set the example. If we want children to think for themselves, we must encourage this by listening to their ideas and treating them with respect. If we genuinely think we always know best, we probably should not be teaching anyway … Are their parents respected and welcomed in the school? If they are not, what are we communicating to the children about the way we view them and their families? The way teachers treat each other and their attitude to the non-teaching staff of the school are all factors influencing the way children will regard the adults around them. (p. 146)

Passion and caring in teaching

Day (2004) acknowledges that to maintain consistently high standards day after day requires something more than mere technical competence; he refers to this 'something special quality' as *passion*. Thus:

> Bringing a passionate self to teaching every day of every week of every school term and year is a daunting prospect. Having a good idea about what to do in the classroom is only the beginning of the work of teaching. It is the translation of passion into action that embodies and integrates the personal and the professional, the mind and the emotion, that will make a difference in pupils' learning lives. (p.14)

Similarly, Winkley (2002) argues that passion requires a long-term commitment and an intensity of interest by teachers in the pupils and the subjects they are teaching. It 'acts as an inner fire, burning away' (p. 23). He also offers a perspective on the importance of a secure and genuine pupil–adult relationship, insisting that a passionate teacher may be quiet and fastidious, just as she or he may be tough and vigorous; but the pupils know about teachers who are committed to them, and forgive them a lot. Such caring is signalled in a large number of small matters, including the way that the teacher speaks to children, looks at them and marks their work. Such a caring attitude not only makes the teacher feel and work better but also oils the relationships in the classroom and enhances self-worth. However, Winkley asserts that part of the unwritten agreement between the teacher and the children is that pupils have to respond reasonably and do their best.

Find out more by reading

Cole, M. (2007) *Professional Attributes and Practice*, London: David Fulton.
Potts, B. (2004) *The Primary Teacher's Pocketbook*, Winchester: Teacher's Pocketbooks.

Part 2

Teaching and learning

Chapter 5

Helping children to love learning

The content of Chapter 5 includes:

- understanding the brain's effect on learning and teaching
- visual, auditory and kinaesthetic styles of learning and forms of teaching
- the meaning and significance of personalised learning
- the importance of play in social, emotional and intellectual development
- making use of the outdoor environment to enrich learning
- deepening learning through thinking, reflecting, mental challenges, reading aloud, poetry and music.

Points to consider as you read this chapter:

1 How your knowledge of brain function influences the way you organise for learning and teaching.
2 Ways to ascertain a pupil's preferred learning style and incorporate the information into your teaching approach.
3 The best way to employ adult help and computer technology to address children's specific learning needs.
4 The educational and social purpose of play.
5 The practicalities of organising outdoor learning and the opportunities it presents for cross-curricular links.
6 Ways to ensure that learning is reinforced and enriched.

Understanding the brain

An important factor in recognising ways in which children learn is to understand brain function. Studies strongly suggest that one side of the brain is normally dominant: if the left side of the brain dominates, the person is likely to be analytical in his or her approach, whereas if the right side dominates, the person can be described as holistic or global. Thus, a left-brain orientated pupil prefers to learn in a step-by-step sequential format, initially concentrating on the fine details and working towards a conceptual understanding of the skill; such an approach can be described as *inductive*, i.e. evidence is gathered from a lot of detail to create a general principle. By contrast, dominance of the right side of the brain means that the pupil prefers to learn by starting with the general concept and then working out the specific details; such an approach can be described as *deductive*, i.e. knowledge in different contexts are 'deduced' from the key principle. Specifically, a person with a right-sided inclination tends to be more random, intuitive and subjective than the left-sided person, preferring to look at the whole picture rather than the individual parts. The dominance of left or right sides of the brain and their accompanying outcomes mean that children – indeed, all of us – tend to think and learn in different ways. Thus, in any group or class of children there will be evidence of different learning characteristics as pupils develop and cultivate ways of responding to their experiences and the information presented to them.

Other useful insights from studies of the brain include the fact that the prime time for *language development*, including learning to talk, is from birth until the end of primary school; children are acquiring language during this entire period but particularly so during the first few years of life. Children therefore benefit from hearing adults talk, sing and read to them during these formative years and affirming the children's attempts to use and create different language forms (notably, speaking and writing; see Eke and Lee, 2008). *Spatial-temporal* reasoning is the expression used in referring to the brain function controlling difficult, complicated tasks like mathematics or playing chess. Such reasoning allows us to imagine ratios and proportions; for example, it helps younger children to understand that vessels of different proportions but the same volume hold the same amount of water.

The development of *emotional and social development* in children, which incorporate capacities such as trust, sensitivity, empathy ('getting alongside') and sympathy are especially important in the years up to adolescence. Early nurturing is essential if children are to find fulfilment, develop resilience and, it is to be hoped, experience genuine happiness. If children are deprived of an intimate relationship with adults and their peers during the years preceding formal schooling, they will probably struggle later on to form suitable human attachments and may have difficulty in making friends and being part of a group. As the part of the brain that regulates emotion is shaped early on through life experiences and fashioned inside and outside school by regular interaction with others, so-called 'emotional intelligence' – the ability to be at ease with oneself and relate to others appropriately – is critical to life success.

Social development occurs in stages and relies on emotional maturation; by the time they attend school, all children should have learned how to share with and support others, and understand the importance of health and safety. It is unquestionably true that parents' efforts to nurture and guide their children during the first few years of life have considerable implications for the work of adults in school with new school entrants. Such an important reality also reinforces the need for teachers of nursery and reception-age children in particular to engage with parents and encourage them in their demanding and vital work of childrearing.

Extend your thinking

By the time most people qualify as teachers, their brains are only about half as active as when they began school as four or five year olds. What can have happened during the intervening time?

Visual, auditory and kinaesthetic learning and teaching

Children benefit from experiencing a variety of teaching approaches, though some of them are more beneficial than others, depending on the child; it is therefore essential to consider the way that pupils learn best. This inclination in learning is often clustered under the general heading of 'learning types', which can for simplicity be divided into three broad categories:

- *Visual* (learn best by seeing).
- *Auditory* (learn best by hearing).
- *Kinaesthetic* (learn best by doing).

Some authors add a further category: *Read/write (R)* – indicating a preference for information displayed as words – to create the acronym VARK. Not surprisingly, more academic pupils have a strong preference for this modality, emphasising text-based input and output expressed through reading and writing in their various forms. The more commonly used three-category preference is known by the acronym, VAK, and each learning 'style' can be broadly characterised as follows:

Visual learners tend to

- look for visual clues and make comments such as 'I see' and 'That looks good to me'
- speak quite rapidly and use numerous hand gestures
- enjoy writing, drawing pictures and diagrams
- suggest imaginative possibilities.

Auditory learners tend to

- say things like, 'That rings a bell' and 'I hear what you're saying'
- enjoy hearing a formal presentation

- sit upright and look straight ahead
- explain what they have learned to someone else.

Kinaesthetic learners will sometimes

- make remarks of the sort, 'Let me have a go' and 'I can't follow what you are saying'
- show spasmodic attentiveness
- fidget and have short concentration spans
- like to make things and use objects for imaginative purposes.

By contrast, children who are not inclined to learn visually may daydream when asked to observe something and fail to spot important details. Children who are not auditory learners may become easily distracted and start whispering, doodling or communicating with a friend. Non-kinaesthetic learners stand back when invited to volunteer, allow others in the group to dominate the resources and (in the case of young children) may resist doing messy activities.

Children normally learn best using a combination of these learning types, so as a teacher you need to organise your teaching in such a way that it takes account of an individual's learning tendencies, though not to do so obsessively. In fact it is a mistake to label children as snugly fitting one of the VAK categories, for the following reasons. First, labelling of any kind is rarely helpful in school unless it is done with the express understanding that it is to assist in providing relevant experiences and not to artificially restrict the child's potential for learning. For example, if you note that Becky responds particularly well to pictures and diagrams, it is correct to identify that she has a tendency to benefit from visual stimuli but incorrect to conclude that she is therefore incapable of concentrating on explanations or discovering practical solutions. Second, children respond differently with different teachers and in different circumstances. The child whose mind wanders quickly with teacher A may concentrate for much longer with teacher B. Similarly, a child who reacts badly to the echoing speech in a school hall during a PE session may be comfortable in the same room during assembly when the bodies absorb and soften sound. Third, it is possible to be over-sensitive to the assumed learning 'style' of each child and artificially distort your teaching to accommodate what you imagine are their specific needs. If taken to extremes, such an approach can be unsettling for you and the children. For example, Franklin (2006) rightly argues that every pupil can benefit from visual images:

> Pupils watch and learn through the image, moving and still. Therefore it is important that teachers use a range of visual images in their teaching to stimulate learning for *all* pupils, rather than to focus on what they might consider to be visually able pupils. (p. 84, original emphasis)

The last thing that any educator wants to hear is a child saying that he doesn't bother listening to instructions because he has been told he is a kinaesthetic learner and his friend insisting that she isn't interested in drawing diagrams and pictures because she is an auditory learner.

Extend your thinking

A sizeable minority of the children in your class suffer from temporary hearing impairment (deafness). When a child apparently isn't listening there may be a physical cause.

It is the common experience of teachers that certain children tend to respond to particular learning stimuli more positively than to others. Some children benefit greatly from what they see (Visual), others can sit and concentrate for a long time when being addressed (Auditory); and yet others learn from 'hands-on' (Kinaesthetic) experiences. In reality, every child – indeed, every learner of whatever age – benefits from a combination of approaches. It is probably more helpful for you to think of these three styles as representing *teaching* approaches rather than the somewhat perplexing expression, 'learning style'. In so doing, you can plan any phase of your teaching (e.g. the introduction, task management, review of lesson, etc.) in one of the following ways:

- You talk all the time and the children listen (auditory).
- You talk but use visual aids to explain or illustrate a point (auditory, visual).
- You use visual aids as the basis for teaching and refer to them regularly when you are talking (visual, auditory).
- You talk or demonstrate a technique and invite different children to offer their ideas (interactive auditory).
- You demonstrate a technique, explain its significance and invite children to step forward and practically assist with its working (visual, auditory, kinaesthetic).
- You spend a short time explaining a task and allow maximum time for children to actively explore (auditory, kinaesthetic).
- You explain the task, allow children time to actively explore it, and encourage feedback from them (auditory, kinaesthetic, auditory).

The above descriptions are only a sample of possible approaches, but you should note that while some of them emphasise a single element, most of them contain a mixture of two or more elements in differing measures. In determining your approach it is important to put yourself in the children's place and ask about the relevance of your teaching method for them with reference to their age, experience and aptitude. Thus, whereas very young children might struggle to absorb too much spoken information, older pupils are able to conceptualise from speech more easily and can process the ideas in a way that infants find difficult. Some subject areas lend themselves to one approach more than to another; for example, science, design and technology, craft and shape-and-space aspects of mathematics will normally require the application of practical skills. You may want children to actively explore a theme through play or using a variety of materials in craft and provide them with considerable freedom to do so; on the other hand you may organise practical activities and select the equipment and strictly define the procedures: do this and then do that. In both cases the children would have exposure to 'kinaesthetic learning' but their experiences would differ considerably with respect to the degree of freedom of choice and their autonomy in decision-making.

When employing visual means you might, for instance, use a large, interesting photograph or a relevant object or a number of unusual items to stimulate curiosity and engage children's interest. The opening phase of the lesson would probably involve you in introducing the topic (i.e. using an auditory form of teaching) then showing the objects or picture to the class (combining visual with some auditory) and perhaps allowing selected children to touch the item and comment on what they see (combining kinaesthetic and auditory). It is commonly the case that when a teacher produces something strongly visual, it elicits a spontaneous and active response from pupils; so don't be surprised at an explosion of remarks, laughter or gasps of wonder. You may want to point out aspects pertaining to the visual aid or invite the children to contribute suggestions; you may want to ask specific questions about the object that children can answer by their close observation; on the other hand, you may want them to speculate about its uses, origin or potential or express their feelings about its qualities. As the lesson unfolds, you will have to make numerous other decisions, such as:

- Should I retain control of the equipment or pass the items around the group for children to touch and feel (with the inevitable delays and the need for close monitoring) or invite one child at a time to come up and handle the object (which allows for greater control but slows the lesson pace)?
- Should I send the children to sit down at tables and speak to them about the task once they are seated; or should I organise everything before they sit down or provide written instructions for children to use with a TA?
- Should I provide a closely pre-determined structure for working (such as an activity sheet) or leave the task more open-ended and introduce a problem-solving approach? For example, to investigate how many ways the object might be useful in the home – in which case a longer period of time will be needed.

In the light of the above examples it is clear that there are numerous practical considerations to consider when deciding the best VAK-related teaching approach to adopt. For instance, if you use a visual aid of small size, children that are furthest away may struggle to see and either complain or shuffle forward or simply not bother to attend. Computerised images on a large screen are useful in many teaching situations but they do not, of course, allow the children to learn by first-hand experience – touching, testing, smelling and so forth. Crucially, in every situation it is vitally important that your speech is consistently clear and easy on the ear: careful articulation of words and a measured pace are essential features of effective teaching.

Strengthening practice

Value and build on what children *can* do rather than spending all your time trying to rectify the things that they *cannot* do.

Personalised learning

One phrase that has wormed its way into the education vocabulary in recent years is 'personalised learning', which refers broadly to ensuring that teaching is responsive to the different ways that pupils learn best. It is posited on a philosophy that it is possible to assess children's progress accurately and tailor-make teaching such that it meets those needs and allows for regular 'assessment for learning' (AFL), thereby directly addressing identified learning needs. Setting aside questions about the doubtful validity of such a grand claim, personalised learning is a useful reminder to teachers and school leaders that a child's individual needs should not be overlooked in the process of whole-class teaching, maintaining pace or fulfilling the immediate curriculum requirements. The implications for teachers are fourfold:

1   using strategies to identify learning needs and subsequently provide adult assistance for children with similar needs in small groups; or individually coached
2   ensuring that exceptionally able pupils (sometimes referred to as 'gifted and talented') are given opportunity to engage with more demanding tasks in that subject area that stretch their capabilities
3   considering more imaginative ways of setting and grouping pupils; for instance, rotating pairs for different activities and intensive coaching for clusters of pupils who struggle with the same learning
4   paying particular attention to pupils from home backgrounds where they may not receive adequate support and encouragement. This element of provision has to be handled very sensitively and may involve nothing more than a TA 'looking out' for the child and offering discrete support to complete tasks and the ensuing praise that will provide security and encouragement.

Most schools have close links with parents whose children require special assistance in their learning or behaviour or both, and there are usually agreed policies in place for contacting and working with them, including partnership 'contracts' between home and school.

The role of teaching assistants (in particular) and other professionals (occasionally) is highly significant if personalised learning is to be anything more than an aspiration. You may discover that some schools have created leadership roles or teaching posts to manage and disseminate best practice in support of the personalised learning agenda, including information to parents and opportunities for them to receive advice about how they may better contribute towards their children's education. Many schools use *peer mentoring* (child to child) or setting up 'buddy' systems that enable older pupils to link with younger ones and support them in their learning (in reading, for instance) and general well-being (e.g. during break times) with a TA having general oversight. Some schools initiate 'vertical tutoring' structures that are based on a mix of pupil ages, such that children can forge supportive relationships outside their own class and year group, a practice that reflects to an extent what happens in the playground. Schools now hold a lot of assessment information about children in their management systems that are available to staff and (in simplified form) to parents, providing information about measurable pupil attainment that can be valuable in planning for personalised learning.

Terminology check

The official definition of *personalised learning* is

> maintaining a focus on individual progress, in order to maximise all learners' capacity to learn, achieve and participate. This means supporting and challenging each learner to achieve national standards and gain the skills they need to thrive and succeed throughout their lives. Personalising learning is not about individual lesson plans or individualisation, where learners are taught separately or largely through a one-to-one approach. (p. 5)

> Training and Development Agency, TDA (2007)
> *Professional Standards for Teachers (Qualified Teacher Status)*

Extend your thinking

All teachers should try to develop the following characteristics in pupils:

- awareness of self ... by being thoughtful and considerate
- awareness of others ... by weighing the impact of words and actions
- open-mindedness ... by genuinely considering alternatives
- a desire to help others ... by exercising responsibility
- eagerness to seek knowledge ... by showing determination
- confidence to seek advice ... by articulating needs clearly
- co-operation as a group member ... by contributing and engaging with others
- willingness to offer suggestions ... by risking ideas
- supporting others ... by valuing everyone's efforts
- courtesy without fawning ... by appropriately respectful behaviour
- decisiveness without rudeness ... by being pleasantly assertive
- selflessness ... by promoting an 'all for one and one for all' attitude.

The importance of play

Play has long been recognised as essential for children's development – socially, emotionally and intellectually – and is one of the most powerful opportunities that children have for trying out and mastering new skills, concepts and experiences. Play helps children to shape appropriate responses to the challenges they encounter in school and contributes to the way that children view themselves as learners. As they play, children resolve complex issues by creating new solutions and ideas, thereby experiencing the empowerment associated with the autonomy to resolve problems. However, in some classes, children view play only as a reward to complete a piece of writing or mathematics, which may downgrade its status.

Some educationists are concerned that young children are being prevented from engaging in traditional forms of spontaneous play as they and their teachers are under excessive pressure to achieve well in the national tests, which are wholly 'paper-based'. For instance, Year 1 teachers might dispense with sand, water and role-play to free-up space and time for more formal, teacher-initiated activities. One way to enhance the significance of play is to resist emphasising assessable achievement and orientate towards a more nurturing approach, fostering imagination and discovery to create a high level motivation for learning. Some structuring of play can be helpful to stimulate children who have difficulty playing. However, regimented play activities can have negative consequences on the social and emotional development of a child because they take away a child's initiative and freedom of choice if they are too organised. By contrast, play that is child-initiated encourages creative and multi-sensory development.

Studies about the value of play are in agreement about the problems associated with a lack of opportunity to do so. Thus:

- Children who are prematurely pushed into regimented academic instruction display less creativity and enthusiasm for learning than their peers who have been given ample time to play.
- Children who memorise isolated facts early in life without opportunity to explore them imaginatively do not develop good long-term retention.
- Children who are deprived of play struggle to develop social and emotional skills that are critical for long-term educational and personal success.

If the above claims are correct, it makes educational sense to have space in the day for younger pupils, in particular, to interact naturally with one another (i.e. without imposed adult structures) as there is a power that comes from ongoing human relationships in which both mind (the intellect) and heart (the emotions) combine in learning. It might appear to an uninformed observer that children at play are wasting their time and not engaged with anything purposeful but it is worth granting children some unscheduled time on their own and with other children, such that they are able to be spontaneous, diversify and deepen their understanding of the social world and develop strategies for coping with emotional challenges and accommodating other people's perspectives.

Although similar principles hold if you are teaching older pupils, a number of practical and developmental considerations apply. First, opportunities for unstructured interaction are severely constrained by the timetable and the requirement to follow a national curriculum and embrace Government-initiated strategies for teaching mathematics and literacy. Second, although even the most sophisticated older pupils are still maturing, they have greater awareness of the social order and their place in it than their younger siblings; the deep imaginings of childhood are replaced by a far more pragmatic (and sometimes sceptical) view of life. Pupils' need for acceptance by peers grows markedly as they grow up; some children are popular, confident and self-sufficient; others reluctantly accept their lowly standing in the social order and search for consolation by creating loose affiliations with other unpopular children or retreating into their lonely and isolated worlds. By contrast with the free-play opportunities offered to new entrants and reception age children, teachers tend to exploit junior age pupils' creative potential through organised activities – especially in drama, design and technology, ICT, art and imaginative forms of writing. Opportunities for 'free' expression of ideas and spontaneity are in a controlled environment, such as circle time, discussions about a topic selected in advance by the teacher or as part of a curriculum topic.

The word 'play' can also refer to 'playing with' electronic games, which has raised considerable controversy in recent years. Although there may be some benefits to these activities, such as improved hand-eye co-ordination, there is growing concern that children spend too much time on sedentary, solitary pursuits that can inhibit their mental and physical well-being. Play in which it is the outcome that motivates the participation tend to train a child's thought patterns and possibly hinder the establishment and maturation of their thought processes. Despite the intensive debate and allegations that electronic games can become addictive and cause children to become detached from reality, it is quite likely that carefully chosen computer games will be used in upper Key Stage 2 classrooms as learning tools.

Children's spontaneous or organised activities during the official break times from class work ('recess') are also referred to as 'play'. Due to a larger number of physically disabled children being educated in mainstream schools, it is important to be sensitive to their particular needs and the organisational, social and physical barriers that might affect their inclusion. These issues are likely to be brought to the fore in the playground area when there is lighter adult supervision (Woolley, 2007).

Strengthening practice

Learn to distinguish between adult-directed and adult-initiated play and the implications for organising and managing the session.

The value of the outdoors to playing and learning

The 'outdoors' includes any space that is not confined within the physical building of the school or educational setting (e.g. nursery) and it is now a requirement that under-fives have access to outdoor play, with suitable equipment and appropriate supervision. Over and above this provision, the school grounds offer all kinds of opportunities to enhance the curriculum, raise pupil motivation and promote cross-subject learning. Developing garden areas, pond projects and environmental studies also teach children the importance of stewardship and conservation and offer a chance to acquire firsthand, multi-sensory knowledge of the natural world. Before traffic increased in volume and speed, streets were places that provided a common space for children's activities, where they learned to interact with others; be initiated into cultural norms; confront boundaries of behaviour; and expend pent-up energy. However, many schools have reduced the amount of break time as a means of reducing supervision costs and anti-social behaviour; furthermore, few places remain for children to play in many urban areas and gardens are much smaller than in the past. Public playgrounds, even though meant for children, are not always well designed, maintained or supervised. School playgrounds are typically limited to combinations of asphalt, turf, and some large structures (such as low level climbing equipment) though a lot of money and effort has been directed towards improving the play environment, not least because poorly designed and maintained play areas are unattractive and depressing venues for children. There is some evidence to suggest that a richly provisioned outdoor area reduces the level of aggressive play. To add to the complexity, the attractions of staying inside when at home – sophisticated technological equipment, large-screen televisions, comfortable rooms and the need to complete homework – act as a disincentive to leave the house. Opportunities for outdoor experiences have therefore become more vital than ever.

Some pupils are demotivated by the traditional academic style of learning and need other forms of stimuli if they are going to progress. In particular, unsettled children (see Chapter 6) are often more relaxed and contented when they move beyond the confines of the classroom into the outdoors. For all pupils, however, it is preferable to view educational visits and trips as being important in their own right, rather than as a reward for good behaviour. Visiting museums, galleries and exhibitions, together with more physical outdoor activities, should be a normal part of the school curriculum, as a lot of informal learning and social bonding takes place during such occasions. Unfortunately, owing to the combined effect of legislation, form filling and fears of litigation should an accident occur during the trip, there has been a fall-off in the number of educational visits taking place beyond the immediate confines of the school grounds in recent years. Teachers are especially concerned about risk factors such as crossing roads; deep and fast-flowing water; slips, trips and falls; sunstroke; insect bites and pollution.

As a trainee, if you want to take children beyond the boundaries of the school grounds, you must operate alongside a qualified teacher. There are well-established procedures even for organising something as apparently simple as a walk to a local park or shopping precinct. Your in-school tutor/mentor will advise you and answer any specific queries, but it is still essential to consider factors such as:

- basic health and safety requirements; correct footwear; complete first-aid kit; a sufficient number of adults per child; explaining your expectations about behaviour; a charged mobile (cell) phone and a list of contact numbers
- man-made hazards, especially dangerous roads and traffic
- natural hazards such as inclement weather and deep or turbulent water
- the demands upon children of extended and unaccustomed physical activity
- protection against specific hazards; for example, using protective gloves and goggles when chipping rocks.

It is always worth visiting the site or venue beforehand and making what is commonly referred to as a 'risk assessment', though 'safety check' is an equally apt expression. Even very local visits have to be carefully timed, especially if they are likely to coincide with break times or the end of the school day; parents get understandably annoyed if children are not on time leaving school and there may be other factors involved with lateness, such as needing to catch a bus, crossing a road after the patrol person has finished or (for older pupils) being unavailable to escort a younger brother or sister home. As with most aspects of the teacher's role, foresight and thorough planning will help you avoid elementary mistakes and keep the children and your reputation intact.

Strategies for deepening learning

It is difficult to believe that pupils can spend years in school listening to the teacher, doing the work set for them and even gaining high grades or marks in formal tests, yet have only a superficial understanding of the areas of learning with which they have engaged. It is possible for beginner teachers to convince themselves that children are 'making good progress' when what is *really* happening is that they are complying with adults' wishes and completing tasks as requested – but never being immersed in learning. For instance, 8-year-old children may be taught how to compose and set out a formal letter to someone important, yet might fail to realise that the letter: (a) will be read by a 'real' person, (b) may be shared with others, (c) will have to be interpreted by the reader, (d) may effect change, such as inducing a written or verbal response from the recipient. In this example, the technical ability to write and compose the letter can be achieved successfully (with the appropriate tick on a record sheet) but the implications have not been fully explored. The following strategies will assist in deepening pupil learning.

Deepening learning through thinking and reflection

Smidt (2006) comments: 'We see how children everywhere develop a range of strategies as problem-solvers, and in doing this make hypotheses, try these out, analyse what happens, identify patterns, generate rules, use analogy, come to conclusions and move on' (p. 107). However, in the hurry-scurry of planning, teaching and assessing, it is easy to get caught on a treadmill of activity and intense concentration and ignore Smidt's shrewd observation. Without realising it you succeed in exhausting the children and yourself! Do not mistake busyness for effectiveness. If you want children to be reflective and provide a classroom environment that is conducive to thoughtfulness, you must model the approach by contemplating and interrogating issues. Although children enjoy sessions that have pace and vitality, they also need opportunities to pause, consider and process the information. In doing so, make sure that you give them something specific to think about; if you merely ask children to 'think' it is likely that most of them will daydream or sit there blankly. If, on the other hand, you ask them to think about (say) the best option, the way that something might be improved or how the story could end, you are giving them an anchor and focus for their thoughts.

When we invite children to express and explore their beliefs we allow the opportunity for further inquiry, so we must be willing to discuss things that directly pertain to children's lives or find ways to connect the subject matter that we teach to children directly. It is one thing to talk about interesting words in a piece of text, it is quite another to use them in a humorous poem about a familiar situation such as a party, an outing, playing in the park or making friends.

To value an enquiry-based approach to learning, pose questions that require concentrated thought or even questions for which there is no immediate answer. For instance, it is appropriate to ask children to choose a favourite lunch box motif; but to encourage deeper thinking you need to ask about why they made the choice, why boys and girls seem to have different preferences or even why the boxes have motifs at all.

Reflection is not to be confused with fantasising – though there is a place for fantasy – or daydreaming. For instance, some pupils have to be confronted and challenged about their own attitude and behaviour, especially towards others. Opportunities for children to think about the effect they have on their classmates and friends should be seized and exploited, not for the purpose of humiliation or inducing guilt, but as a means of helping children to be more aware of the impact and implications of their actions. For instance, it is essential that children are alerted to the consequences of apparently minor, harmless actions. Thus, rubbish thrown on to the floor has to be cleared up by *someone*; an unkind word can cause the recipient unhappiness that lasts well beyond the moment it is said; failure to meet a deadline means that someone else is inconvenienced, and so forth. Although a few children wilfully exploit situations, the majority of younger children especially are largely unaware of the consequences of their actions. As Sedgwick (2008) wisely comments about the basis for teaching philosophy/thinking: 'Everyone has to believe that children have that sense of wonder, and also that sense that the unexamined life is not worth living' (Introduction).

Strengthening practice

When you give children opportunity to think about something specific, make it more interesting by asking them to indicate their feelings about the issue by suggesting a score on a scale from 1 to 5. The number they choose is less important than the degree of involvement it elicits.

Deepening learning by regular mental challenges

Offering choices to pupils; allowing them to make their own decisions; asking them searching questions; providing materials for play and facilitating exploratory activity, all help to stimulate attentive concentration on their part. Similarly, the use of quizzes, puzzles, team games, walks around the local district and treasure trails, all assist in nurturing the development of a more secure attention span and increased enthusiasm for learning. Even common activities such as dominoes, cards, dice games and matching up pictures are helpful methods to develop a child's memory and concentration. For older primary age pupils, 'consequence' games such as draughts or chess can be introduced into the classroom, thereby encouraging the child to think ahead and employ effective strategies, rather than relying on instinct.

The use of so-called mental/oral time at the start of mathematics sessions is one formal opportunity to extend children's thinking, but there are informal occasions when you can excite their interest by spontaneously posing questions, especially speculative ones to which there is no immediate answer and that require careful consideration. Aim to make your classroom a slightly unpredictable place – though not chaotic, of course – where the children never quite know what is coming next. Perhaps you can bring in an odd-looking mysterious object one day and ask them to offer suggestions about its origin; or stir their imaginations by playing a recorded sound as a forerunner to using a kaleidoscope of colours to create a painting; or wear a very unusual brooch with 'magic powers' that can grant three wishes; or give the children Viking names and build a drama lesson around the characters; or ask a player from a local sports team to come into school and join in with the games session before responding to pupil questions; or even hire a cartoon character full-dress set for a day, as a stimulus for children's imaginative writing.

Mental challenges are most appropriate when they relate to genuine situations and require children to think beyond the predictable level and try to extend the boundaries of possibility. The principle of 'think big and then think small' captures the notion that it is worth encouraging children to adopt a 'scattergun' approach initially, in which you allow them first to make bold, even idiosyncratic ('wacky') suggestions. After exhausting their store of ideas, they can concentrate on 'thinking small' by taking the suggestions and examining them in detail to produce more realistic and workable solutions and deepen their understanding.

Strengthening practice

Every week or two put up a sheet of paper with a child-friendly statement on it. Children put a tick or write their names in one of three columns: (a) Yes, I agree, (b) No, I do not agree, (c) I am not sure. Older children can be invited to write a short comment. At the end of the week share the results with the children and, if relevant, discuss the issues. An example of a statement suitable for very young children might be: 'Does Teddy look better dressed in blue than in red?' accompanied by a picture. An example of a statement for older children might be: 'Should adverts be banned during children's TV?'

Deepening learning by reading aloud and telling stories

Numerous studies about reading aloud to children point to the unmistakable conclusion that it assists neural (brain) development, increases their knowledge of the world, extends their vocabulary and their familiarity with written language ('book language') and their interest in reading. It also builds listening skills and the ability to concentrate at length. Reading aloud and telling stories assists in developing children's ability to express themselves more confidently, easily and clearly in spoken and, almost certainly, in written terms. As they listen to the stories, children's natural curiosity and imagination can be unleashed. Stories – like play – help to expand children's horizons, calm their fears and expose them to new situations and a range of perspectives. Reading picture books promotes a young child's appreciation for the arts through exposure to different styles of pictures and illustrations. The discipline required to sit and listen also aids the development of appropriate behaviour and building social cohesion. Reading aloud to children will not, in itself, create readers, but it contributes to a book-loving culture and establishes in children's minds an enthusiasm for the printed word as they associate it with intimacy, enjoyment and an opportunity to exercise their imaginations.

Similarly, the use of poetry is useful in teaching a variety of important skills and enthusing children. Linking poetry with other areas of the curriculum (such as drama) and increasing pupils' confidence through public speaking and choral speaking – whereby children speak in unison and echo each phrase or line as spoken by the teacher (including imitating the intonation and volume of the teacher's speech) – all help to enliven this area of the curriculum. Innovative use of poetry also involves memorising, interpreting the written text, considering the author's purpose in writing the poem and imitating the style in their own writing.

Extend your thinking

Imagination is like a muscle in the mind. It needs proper feeding and regular exercise to help it grow.

Strengthening practice

Tell pupils to imagine that during a sea trip together they are shipwrecked on a desert island. Provide a map of the island showing key places, such as cliffs, caves, forest and other landmarks. Ask small groups to make up a story about 'what happened next'. Do not allow them to record their ideas but to rely solely on memorising the facts of their discussion. Share the ideas during a plenary time, using a variety of presentational forms: verbal feedback, mime, 'stick-man' pictures, etc. Invite constructive comments as each group discloses its story.

Deepening learning through listening to music

The prospect of classical music as a device for enhancing intellect and stimulating development fascinates educators and parents, and there have been numerous claims over recent years that it can have positive effects on children's development and health. Studies in the early 1990s suggested that pupil scores on spatial-temporal reasoning tests improve by up to one-third after listening to classical music, notably from classical composers like Mozart. Although these claims are disputed, it is certainly true that music provides opportunity for children to be liberated from their immediate situation and employ their imaginations to enter a brighter and fairer place of joy and contentment. It can also serve to inspire, uplift and release creativity.

It is also possible that background music assists in *developing memory*, as memory recall tends to improve when the music played during learning is then played when trying to remember the relevant facts. This phenomenon is based on the principle that knowledge is associated with forms of music in much the same way that a scent will trigger memories of particular events or occasions. The benefit to a pupil's *attention span* of listening to music is less clear. You can enhance the use of music in the classroom through strategies such as:

- using dance, with the children expressing themselves physically by stomping, marching, swaying, jumping and shaking
- inviting children to hum and sing along with music to enhance their language development skills
- developing motor and rhythmic skills by encouraging children to invent their own instruments from classroom materials or recycled objects and perform for or with the rest of the class
- highlighting a composer each month by providing brief biographical information and playing extracts from his or her work.

See Jones and Robson (2008) for more detailed suggestions about classroom practice.

Another reason that every child must be exposed to a range of music is that it forms part of the fabric of society, such that the intrinsic value of music for each individual is widely recognised in the diverse cultures that contribute to the world as children experience it. Indeed, every human culture group uses music to promote its ideas and ideals. Even the fact that children have different musical preferences can act as a prompt for analysing likes and dislikes; don't be surprised if some pupils have very strong and entrenched feelings about the subject.

Terminology check

Spatial means pertaining to, or involving, or having the nature of space.

Temporal means of, relating to, or limited by time.

Spatial-temporal reasoning is the ability to visualise spatial patterns and mentally manipulate them over a time-ordered sequence. In practice, it means an ability to envision and rotate images in the mind. Visual thinkers are most likely to be efficient in spatial-temporal reasoning.

Strengthening practice

Have a 'music moment' every day lasting for a few minutes during registration or after lunch. Do not attempt to 'analyse' the piece. Instead, ask children to rate their enjoyment under simple headings, such as:

- It made me sad.
- It made me feel glad.
- It did not make me feel any different.

And invite them to finish the sentence *'The music makes me think about ... '* Alternatively, use music as a two-minute stimulus for stretching, moving or dancing. Call the time 'mad music' or 'wacky wiggles' or 'bounce to the beat' to emphasise its fun side.

Professional learning perspectives

The brain and learning

Caine and Caine (1994) offer 12 principles for brain-based learning. A selected summary of their ideas is presented below.

1 The brain is always doing many things at once, such that thoughts, emotions, imagination and predispositions operate simultaneously. Good teaching shapes the learner's experience so that all these aspects of brain operation are addressed.
2 There can be a five year difference in maturation between any two supposedly 'average' children, so that academic attainment cannot be anticipated solely on the basis of the child's age.
3 The learning environment needs to provide stability and familiarity through routine classroom behaviours and procedures. At the same time, provision must be made to satisfy pupil curiosity and hunger for novelty, discovery and challenge, and invite children to make choices by using real-life contexts where possible.
4 The brain attempts to discern and understand patterns as they occur and expresses unique and creative patterns of its own through problem solving,

critically thinking and even daydreaming. It resists having isolated pieces of information imposed on it, unrelated to what makes sense.

5 The emotional climate in the school and classroom must be monitored by giving adequate time for reflection and seeing the 'big picture'. Some of the most significant experiences in a child's life are serendipitous (random) 'moments of truth'.

6 Vocabulary and grammar are best understood and mastered when incorporated in genuine, whole language experiences. Similarly, equations and scientific principles need to be dealt with in the context of living science.

7 Teachers transmit subtle signals to pupils about the importance and value of what is being learned through their own enthusiasm, coaching and modelling. It is important for teachers to be genuine, as the listeners always discern their true inner state.

8 Pupils need to begin to take charge of learning and the development of personal meanings, so they become more aware of their preferred learning style and reorganise information in a way that makes it meaningful and valuable to them.

9 Facts and skills that are dealt with in isolation need a lot of practice and rehearsal. The more separated information and skills are from prior knowledge and actual experience, the more dependence there needs to be on inefficient rote memory and repetition.

10 Teachers need to use a large number of real-life activities, including classroom demonstrations, projects, field trips, visual imagery of certain experiences and best performances, stories, metaphor, drama and interaction of different subjects.

11 Teachers need to create a state of relaxed alertness that combines general relaxation with an atmosphere that is low in threat and high in challenge.

12 Learning changes the structure of the brain, so the more that we learn, the more individual we become. Teaching should be sufficiently flexible to allow children to express visual, tactile, emotional or auditory preferences.

Using poetry imaginatively

Linda Pagett (2007) is an enthusiast for poetry in the classroom but warns that teachers are sometimes nervous about using this medium because of fears about their own ability to teach it. Pagett dismisses such attitudes and argues that:

> Poetry can be powerful – not if it is locked in the pages of an unopened book but if it is read and engaged with. It can enable us to look afresh at fairly mundane things, affect our emotions and make us think. Many texts can do this, but poetry is more memorable and so we have it to hand more easily. It is often figurative and so creates pictures in the mind; the rhythms stay with us and resonate around our heads, so poetry is a form where both visual and aural aspects explore the way that meaning is created. (p. 89)

Pagett offers a variety of practical suggestions about promoting poetry, including:

- learning a favourite poem by heart
- placing poetry posters around the school with sections of poems for children to read
- reading poems aloud (and imaginatively) to children
- using existing models of poems to write one of the same style
- incorporating musical instruments into a performance
- supporting children's engagement through drama and art.

Find out more by reading

Dean, J. (2006) *Meeting the Learning Needs of all Children*, London: Routledge.
Wilmot, E. (2006) *Personalised Learning in the Primary Classroom*, Carmarthen: Crown House.

Behaviour and the twenty-first-century child

The content of Chapter 6 includes:

- ways to enthuse children and light the fire of learning
- developing effective forms of teacher–pupil interaction
- ways to increase pupil attention span
- helping pupils to cope with periods of boredom
- dealing with unsettled children
- common mistakes made by beginner teachers.

Points to consider as you read this chapter:

1   How to focus on children's potential and exploit their readiness to learn as a means of counteracting discipline problems.
2   Methods to extend concentration level and counteract anti-social behaviour.
3   Pre-emptive forms of discipline to employ with restless children and those with extreme forms of behaviour.
4   The need to reflect on practice and reduce errors.

Lighting the fire

We noted in Chapter 5 that children love to learn and, if sufficiently enthused, demonstrate an intense desire to find out more by any available means. In such cases, poor behaviour is not normally an issue. Learning is normally organised into sessions (periods of time that divide up the day) and lessons (timetabled sessions by subject or cross-curricular themes). However, it is possible to be so intent on reaching the end product of task completion that we neglect the *process* of learning through which pupils pass and thereby increase the risk of boredom and restless behaviour.

Terminology check

The word *behaviour* is used in the broad sense of the way in which a person or group responds to a specific set of conditions; it is not just about being 'good' or 'naughty'. *Discipline* describes the action taken by the teacher as a result of a child's inappropriate behaviour.

One of the differences between efficient and effective teaching is that the effective teacher pays as much attention to the process of learning as to the end product. *Efficient* teachers are satisfied if they follow their lesson plan exactly and the children produce neat work, complete the sheet, finish the task, hand in the work and leave the room looking orderly. The *effective* teacher is also interested in such matters but also keen to 'rattle a few cages', risk deviations from the lesson plan if children are keen to know more, invite pupil contributions and delay the instant gratification that children get from completing the task with ease. *Excellent* teachers observe children closely and pick up cues from their responses to breathe energy into the proceedings. Their classrooms may be livelier than those of other teachers, but noise is generated by motivated and stimulated young minds, eager to find out more and push the boundaries of learning. Pupils tumble out of the session, animated and talkative, brimming over with spontaneous enthusiasm. Aim to make at least some of your sessions like that.

Strengthening practice

To invigorate pupils and maintain their interest make small, sudden and unannounced deviations from the lesson direction: make a controversial statement; raise a provocative issue; ask for a class vote about options; make a deliberate mistake; read a short poem; sing a song. But use such moments sparingly; the power lies in their sporadic occurrence.

Children can be wildly enthusiastic for something that touches their hearts and intellects. They have reservoirs of ideas, interests and deep-seated desires that, like the proverbial genie in the bottle, wait impatiently to be released. Their heads are full of fantasies, imaginings and extravagant notions about their own and others' lives. They are easily astonished, brimming with wonder and desperately yearning to uncloak the mysteries that surround them. They will chatter incessantly about their hobbies, friends and pastimes. Their speech is punctuated by expressions of unrestrained joy, moments of exhilaration, contradictions, doubts and (in the case of older pupils) fervent loyalty to an individual or a cause. They bicker, dispute what is said, grapple with uncertainty and strive to make sense of their place in the world. Given opportunity, children will channel their energies into an exploration of things that fascinate and excite them. Watch them burst into action as they are given opportunity to collaborate on a problem-solving exercise. Hear the richness of language as they respond to creative stimuli, share ideas and strain to reach consensus. The job of every teacher, assistant and trainee is to capture this raw energy, harness the cauldron of fervour that lies quietly simmering in each child and provide the spark that produces an eruption of motivation for learning. You will rarely have discipline problems if you do so.

Extend your thinking

Don't plug the lava flow of learning with lesson structures that fail to take account of pupil perspectives and by using lifeless presentations that dampen even the brightest flame. Take the cork out of the bottle.

Strengthening practice

To motivate children, you might invite some street dancers or a Samba drummer to come in to school to perform; help pupils to make video recordings of their own dancing, acting and expressing opinions; produce a class newspaper or a poster advertising the school; create models from everyday items; inspire them to draw or paint illustrations for a story; produce simple puppets to support drama; challenge them to find a simple way to count the number of leaves on the field; write new words for a familiar tune. Light the fire!

Effective teacher–pupil interaction

It almost seems unnecessary to remind you that children behave like children; but they do! They welcome exciting moments and love to chatter, have fun, be adventurous and play with friends. You have the delicate task of shaping behaviour without being oppressive or crushing children's spontaneity and enthusiasm. This balancing act is far more difficult than it appears to an outsider, for whereas most experienced teachers are experts at encouraging pupil contributions without permitting a free-for-all, trainee teachers are sometimes either too uncompromising or too lax initially and then over-compensate by going to the other extreme. A useful analogy is pruning a shrub; if it is done too hard, the plant suffers and takes ages to recover; if too soft, the plant becomes straggly; worst of all, if no action is taken, it does not produce any fruit at all. Only the correct pruning produces a healthy plant and, in due course, results in a proliferation of flowers.

The overarching purpose during pupil–teacher interaction is twofold: first, to encourage well-regulated pupil involvement; second, to offer insights into pupils' understanding and grasp of issues. In other words the interaction between you and the children is not solely about inspiring interest and rein-forcing learning, but also concerned with assessing progress. In this regard the TA can be of immeasurable help as she or he watches the proceedings and makes notes about particular children's responses and actions, with particular reference to misconceptions and misunderstandings. You will, however, need to discuss with the assistant after the session what constitutes a significant pupil reaction; for instance, a child who keeps thrusting a hand in the air may be indicating enthusiasm rather than exhibiting understanding or accurate knowledge.

Judging an acceptable pupil response depends partly on your instincts, partly on the agreed class/school rules but mainly on the purpose of that par-ticular lesson phase. If you are imparting knowledge or asking children to think and ponder an issue, you will probably want them to remain silent and concentrate their full attention on what you are saying. If you are asking sin-gle-answer questions to discover what children remember you will want them to respond as and when you select a pupil to answer. If you ask more probing questions to ascertain the depth of understanding you will probably rely on volunteers ('hands up'). There will also be occasions when you set pupils to work in pairs or small groups initially and report back at a later time, in which case a spokesperson from each group will be required to summarise ideas. In such a situation, you have to decide whether to appoint the person or to allow the group to select an individual. If the purpose is to allow free-ranging discussion, it is essential to clarify the rules of engagement and enforce them consistently (e.g. wait until someone has finished speaking; when you finish speaking put your hand down to indicate such, and so on). One way and another make sure that everyone understands what you expect from them. Here is an example of the sorts of 'rules of engagement' you might want to impose.

Rules of engagement in discussion

- Wait for your turn.
- Speak clearly when it is your turn.
- Look at the person speaking and smile, even if you don't agree.
- Listen carefully to what the person says.
- Allow the person to finish speaking.
- Tell the person that you agree if you agree, and why.

- Tell the person you disagree if you disagree, and why.
- Try to summarise what the other person is saying.
- Use positive language, such as: *That's a nice idea.*
- Work as a team.

In gauging pupil responses, you must also take account of the fact that working closely with a *group* of children raises different issues from working with the *whole class* (see Baines *et al.*, 2008). Group work is more intimate and intensive and tends to invite spontaneity, so you must make it clear to what extent you welcome such behaviour. To deter calling out and help to keep the situation more orderly, get into the habit of saying: *'Put your hand up if...'* before asking a question. Watch that children don't have their hands up for too long and look for other ways of eliciting a response other than an individual pupil answering, such as *'whisper what you think to a friend'* or give an either/or and ask children to select from the options by using a simple voting technique (either the conventional hands-up or a more unusual method, such as those in favour shutting their eyes and those against keeping them open, to a count of three).

Despite the demands of intensively interactive teaching, you may be consoled to know the most productive learning does not usually come from individual tasks (e.g. each child completing a worksheet) but from occasions when there is an exchange of ideas between child and child, or child and adult. Such interactions energise a session but can be difficult to negotiate, as there is a lot for you to think about and manage simultaneously. In the early stages with a new class it is often better to spend more time closely controlling events, rather than facilitating intense interaction or fostering collaboration. *Didactic teaching*, in which you provide nearly all the verbal contribution and have a largely 'passive' audience (i.e. pupils listen but make minimal response unless invited to do so), generally creates fewer discipline problems (assuming that you don't drone on endlessly) but rarely provides the climate for deep learning unless accompanied by opportunities for children to grapple with issues and concepts in subsequent tasks and activities (see Coultas, 2007).

Terminology check

Elicitation is a term used to describe a process by which you try to draw out from children their present knowledge and understanding. The most common elicitation method is through questioning, but elicitation might also involve setting a test, asking children for their ideas (verbally), asking them to draw a picture or diagram to represent their knowledge (a web map) or even acting something out.

Increasing children's attention span

Children are growing up in a society that is bombarded by rapid visual media that has the capacity to reduce healthy attention span development. It is popularly claimed that extensive exposure to television and computer games develops brain systems that tend to *deflect* attention rather than *focus* it. Over recent years there also appears to have been a sharp increase in the number of children with more impulsive behaviours, less willing and able to persevere with challenging mental tasks. A small number of these children are what is termed 'hyperactive' ('exceedingly active') and may react impulsively to external stimuli, such as a comment from another child, a powerful visual image or an attractive item. It is therefore essential that children receive active practice in thinking and learning to build increasingly stronger neural (brain) connections for the simple reason that a mature attention span comes with a mature brain. Forms of active practice might include practical work involving the creation of a 3D or 2D product, verbal responses and decisions that involve selecting from a range of options.

As noted earlier, children's brains continue to develop from and even before birth, and throughout the school years, and attention span is determined in large measure by the type of 'programming' received from external stimuli. Studies suggest that an average child's formal attention span (in minutes) is approximately as long as the age of the child; in other words a five year old can normally only manage five minutes of uninterrupted concentration. Many pupils are used to being immersed in watching TV programmes that are visually compelling – containing battle scenes, fun and frolics, cartoons – but do little to stimulate their minds, make them think, consider options, make decisions, formulate opinions, evaluate merit, and so forth. To maintain interest, programme-makers provide rapid, easily absorbed extracts, flitting across a range of camera shots that are enhanced by multi-media wizardry. Some children become so used to these intensive stimuli that 'one-dimensional' lessons in school that necessitate close attention to the content are viewed as relatively uninspiring. As a result, the teacher may struggle to keep such children on task. In the case of the youngest primary age pupils, even getting some of them to sit still and listen to a story can provide a considerable challenge. You cannot and should not try to compete with multi-media technology, but rather take account in lesson planning of the power and influence of meaningful adult–child interaction.

It is interesting to contrast the *external* control of visual stimuli used by the media to bombard children's senses, with the *internal* control and discipline required by children when participating (for example) in a self-directed play activity or collaborative problem-solving exercise. Under such conditions and within the limits of timetable constraints and teacher direction, the child determines how long he or she will attend to individual tasks, discusses with others the way forward and adjusts to the prevailing social conditions – accommodating quieter or shyer children who may be reluctant to participate. When involved in a group exercise children who are obliged to cope with the ideas and emotional responses from their peers and adjust their speech and actions accordingly. Similarly, when pupils are involved in self-initiated activities – in which they explore their environments and make decisions, talk to themselves and others – they make choices and exercise control rather than having it externally monitored and directed.

By contrast, a constant stream of interruptions (especially visually captivating ones) disengages the *inner dialogue*; that is, the talking that takes place inside the child's head. As a result, concentration and sustained attention become more and more fragmented; the pupil jumps from one activity to another, restlessly seeking the next stimulus 'fix' and unable to persevere to complete a task. Such children no longer construct *personal* meaning and understanding internally through thinking processes and self-talk because their attention has been monopolised by the external source. Consequently, children's attention span diminishes, as they increasingly become spectators as opposed to being active participants in learning.

Increasing pupil resourcefulness

Although the above scenario only applies directly to a small number of pupils, their influence on your ability to maintain an orderly, disciplined learning environment is disproportionately large. However, the reality is that all children are grappling with similar issues as they grow and develop, some of them more successfully than others. To increase children's resourcefulness, you must consider ways in which you can elicit a positive response from them by creating a vibrant learning environment and gradually seduce them into engaging with the regular curriculum. If you have succeeded in creating an atmosphere of trust and security by clarifying your expectations, approachability and supportive feedback, promoting the following strategies will, over time, be beneficial. Thus, from time to time:

GIVE PUPILS OPPORTUNITIES TO PLAN THEIR OWN WORK AND THE WAY THEY TACKLE PROBLEMS

For example, let them decide whether to hand write or word process; allow them to work their way through maths problems beyond the timetabled lesson if they choose to do so.

PRESENT THE PUPILS WITH COMPLEX SCENARIOS THAT OBLIGE THEM TO MAKE CHOICES

For example, a team's best player is injured; during the period of injury the team wins every match. Should the star be reinstated after recovering from the injury?

PROVIDE A SCENARIO THAT REQUIRES PUPILS TO DISCUSS OPTIONS AND DETERMINE THE MOST APPROPRIATE ONE

For example: 'How can we save water while still staying clean and healthy?'

INVITE PUPILS TO MAKE SUGGESTIONS ABOUT KEY WORDS AND PHRASES THAT CAN BE ATTACHED TO A CENTRAL CONCEPT OR IDEA

The concept might be a theme such as 'helpfulness' or 'happiness' or 'politeness'; the idea might be 'tackling bullying' or 'keeping the school grounds clean' or 'making friends'.

RE-VISIT A FAMILIAR TASK THAT THEY FORMERLY TACKLED IN A SYSTEMATIC FASHION AND INVITE THEM TO TRY DIFFERENT SOLUTIONS

For instance, if they had initially classified leaves on the basis of their shape, ask them to think of a different system to organise them.

Quite often the opportunity for discussion is a sufficient spur to activate children's minds and initiate lively forms of talk. Older children are normally capable of discussing a topic in pairs or small groups after the introduction. If so, make sure that you give specific instructions about the expected outcome; for example, whether pupils have to produce a written or visual record or complete a *pro forma* or verbally summarise the group's decisions. More mature pupils can be encouraged to talk for a short time about controversial issues and then offer their ideas to the whole class for consideration; for example, to discuss a topic such as: 'What are the advantages and disadvantages about being educated at home rather than at school?' or 'How can we help children to keep fit?' For all forms of group discussion, it is important to state the time allowed for the interaction (and to give a couple of minutes warning as the period draws to a close). Even if pupils are used to working in this collaborative way, you will need to reassure them that there are a variety of acceptable outcomes (to offset the 'what does the teacher want' tendency). Younger children enjoy a more tangible approach, such as placing a coloured brick in an appropriately designated space on a floor map to indicate preference. For example, they might each be asked to place a brick on either the blue, pink, yellow or green corner to vote for one story to be read to them in preference to another. Such an approach is more demanding than being highly directive and requires perseverance, but it is ultimately more satisfying and beneficial for all concerned.

Strengthening practice

Ask the children to imagine that two friendly visitors from outer space called Blob 22 and Blob 42 arrive at school on their tour of the Universe.

They speak simple English but have never visited Earth before and want to find out as much as they can about us. Depending on their ages, ask the children in pairs or small groups to do some or all of the following:

- Draw the aliens.
- Give them names (they only came with Blob registration numbers).
- Write down some places that you will take them.
- Draw a map so they can explore locally.
- Make lists of Do and Do Not.
- Explore the concept of 'being a stranger' during drama.
- Paint pictures of the aliens' home planet.
- Compose a simple song based on a familiar tune to sing to them.
- Write a letter to the local newspaper about their visit.

Helping pupils to cope with short periods of inactivity

We all remember feeling bored when we were at school and fervently want to avoid the children in our classes suffering a similar fate, so teachers try hard to ensure that the work they provide is interesting and, as far as possible, enjoyable. As such, it is highly desirable that you place a high premium on motivation and a love of learning. However, boredom results from a variety of circumstances:

- because the work is inappropriate
- because the work is too easy or demanding
- because the children have been expected to concentrate on the same thing for too long
- because they prefer to do another activity
- because the teacher is bored.

It pays to be aware of such factors and try to provide a different and more inspirational set of experiences.

Paradoxically, however, the race to create increasingly sophisticated and engaging stimuli – whether technological or other forms – means that we may be denying the children the opportunity to experience and cope with short periods of inactivity. Although it is advisable to keep children busily engaged with the work, there is also a place for silence, where children sit still, reflect on what has been said and control the urge to be active. Stillness is a necessary part of developing intrinsic ('inner') motivation, tapping into one's creative potential, developing the ability to concentrate and allowing ingenuity and inventiveness to emerge. Growth and maturation is, by its very nature, slow and steady, and necessitates an ability to cope with periods of inactivity and self-sufficiency. Don't be afraid of insisting on short periods of 'constructive silence'.

Extend your thinking

Majid, a reception age child, is looking out of the window instead of listening to the teacher's discourse about alliteration. On being asked to pay attention he gasps, 'But, Miss, a plane has just made a long white scratch in the sky!' What is an appropriate response such that you can: (a) maintain the lesson's rhythm; (b) seize the moment; (c) handle Majid's misconception without spoiling his sense of wonder and awe?

Coping with very unsettled children

Children are very unsettled for many reasons: a child may have an innate tendency to be restless or it is a deliberate action to manipulate a situation to advantage or the prevailing learning conditions spark an adverse reaction (e.g. a cramped room). Most children respond positively to the sorts of discipline strategies described elsewhere in this book but many classes contain a number of children who seem immune to standard behaviour management strategies. Such pupils listen when you explain patiently why such and such a form of behaviour is unhelpful then carry on behaving as if they had never heard you; your enthusiastic praise when they behave appropriately is met with indifference; your scolding merely brings blank looks. Using the now-familiar routine of writing their names on the board is ineffective and denying them 'golden time' or time to play brings only tearful frustration. It is not uncommon for the fragile world of very unsettled children to collapse under the weight of emotional tensions that they carry but cannot control. If you make a special effort to be kind and helpful they sometimes take advantage or don't know how to respond appropriately and leave you feeling betrayed. So what can be done?

First, you must fight an instinctive tendency – occasionally fuelled by colleagues' comments – to label children who struggle and distort situations in the ways described above as 'maladjusted' or 'weird'. While they may act wilfully at times it is frequently the case that something in their brains is not wired up correctly and/or their family lives and social experiences have failed to provide necessary security and self-discipline. In recent years it has become common to refer to this group of children as 'having ADHD', where the acronym stands for Attention Deficit and Hyperactivity Syndrome. Sadly, some of these children (the majority of whom are boys) are treated by being given medical drugs to control their behaviour, though deep concern is now being expressed about the possible long-term damage that such an approach might be causing. Not all 'unsettled' pupils have attention deficit *and* hyperactivity: some children struggle to concentrate ('attention deficit'); others are irrepressible ('hyperactivity'); yet others combine the two dimensions, with the inevitable challenging behaviour that follows.

A teacher's responsibility involves structuring life in school and providing a discipline framework within which unsettled children can gradually develop acceptable behaviour, as only after the behaviour has improved can you ascertain if the short attention span is a learned response (i.e. the child has not been encouraged to persevere) or something more psychologically profound. If the problems have their origins in factors outside school (such as poor parenting), the involvement of other agencies (such as Social Services) may be appropriate. In the meantime, specific interventions to stretch the child's attention span can be initiated to improve listening and encourage task completion. There are no short cuts to achieving these goals but you can make headway in rectifying the position by providing the right sort of environment for learning. The remainder of this section offers specific advice about how to manage situations involving unsettled or disruptive children, where the problems are largely or wholly innate (due to upbringing or birth factors) rather than wilful (where the child is capable of concentrating and being cooperative but selects not to do so). The following points are relevant.

Provide security

All children need a calm, secure environment, with a regular but flexible routine. Very active children also need special adult help in conforming. Thus, a quiet environment encourages thinking and listening and silent reading; predictable daily events with constant reassurance help to ensure that the child's responses also become more regular. Attention deficit symptoms are made worse by sleep deprivation and hunger, so you should try to check that the child eats and drinks at the proper time and, in some cases, has opportunities for physical rest.

Adopt a positive outlook

It is quite likely – and understandable – that the child will be labelled by his or her peers and by some adults as a 'nuisance' or 'a trouble-maker'. You will need to work hard to convince *yourself* that these pessimistic tags are unhelpful before you can influence the children and your colleagues. Every pupil in your care must feel loved and accepted, even when his or her behaviour does not instantly warrant it. As long as the children have this kind of acceptance and opportunities to gain success in an area that interests them, their sense of self-worth will be strengthened and you will feel that your perseverance is bearing fruit.

Accept the child's limitations

It is important to accept that some children are naturally active and energetic and in all probability will remain so throughout their time in school. Nothing helps a hyperactive child more than having a tolerant, patient teacher, with a reservoir of goodwill and humour. Firm persuasion takes longer than fierce insistence but it is more effective in the long term. Such patience should not be confused, of course, with a pusillanimous, weak-willed approach to the problem. It is also worth noting that when a severely hyperactive child becomes exhausted, his or her self-control often breaks down and the hyperactivity may become more acute. Another characteristic of acutely active children is that some of them appear unable to 'switch off' their minds and may need a familiar source of comfort; for example, hugging a soft toy (younger children) or holding a mascot or prized possession (for older children). Additional classroom assistant support is essential under such extreme circumstances – a mature, unflappable assistant who genuinely enjoys the challenge is particularly valuable.

Provide an outlet for the release of energy

Hyperactive children's pent-up energy cannot be suppressed by dint of your personality or applying restrictive measures. Rather, the bursts of fervour need an outlet, which in the everyday life of the school may be difficult to discover, though regular outdoor activities such as running, sports and nature walks are beneficial. In bad weather the children ideally need a recreational area in which they can play with minimal restrictions and unobtrusive adult supervision. Very lively children gain from having a narrow range of choice of activity because too much choice can be hard for them to cope with. Owing to the pupil's rough handling of equipment, items should be safe and relatively unbreakable.

Promote personal fulfilment

Very active pupils are sometimes desperate to work with one particular classmate and won't settle until they have their 'special friend' as partner. Sadly, the intensive and even obsessive demands can be such that the chosen classmate declines the invitation after a short period of time, leaving the impulsive partner desperate for another companion. You will need to use great wisdom and tact to resolve this type of ongoing situation. Educational visits present a particular challenge and special arrangements may have to be made; the class teacher and SENCO will advise on the matter. Be sure to praise the hyperactive child when he or she works or plays independently, resists interrupting you when you are talking to other children or addressing the class, or remains calm when working in close proximity to other children.

Maintain consistently firm discipline

Rules should be formulated mainly to prevent harm to the restless child and to others. Aggressive behaviour, such as biting, hitting or pushing others (adult or child), should not be accepted in the hyperactive child any more than in the 'normal' child, though you may have to deal with the *results* of such incidents rather than being able to prevent them occurring. While it is important to eliminate aggressive behaviour, you must be wary of imposing unattainable standards, such as insisting that the child sits absolutely still, when such a response exceeds the child's capacity to conform. Excessively active children can only cope with a small number of rules, which should be enforced firmly but kindly. It is best to start with a few clear, fundamental rules and add others gradually. As with all children, it is far better to emphasise and praise positive behaviour, though it is not easy to achieve, especially if you have been struggling with his or her irrational behaviour for long periods of time.

Be explicit

You must not only say what you mean but also mean what you say. In doing so it is essential to be explicit about what sort of actions and behaviour are allowable in the lesson. A few moments spent in outlining the parameters of what is and is not permissible will save you a lot of trouble subsequently, as children understandably become frustrated and anxious if your directions and explanations are vague and ill-defined. The form of explanation that you offer depends to a large extent on the nature of the teaching and learning approach that you are fostering. If the task is principally as a means for you *to determine the children's understanding* of an idea or strategy (how to go about doing something), your explanations are likely to be more heavily procedural; for example: work alone, stay in your seat, put your name at the top, finish as many sums as you can, and so forth. If the purpose is *to encourage children to explore, test and experiment,* your explanations will be weighted towards clarifying boundaries (the limits of what they are allowed to do), offering suggestions about possible approaches (while still leaving them free to select their preferred option where possible) and organisational directives (e.g. about time factors and level of co-operation). The need for clarity also underlines the point that it is important to be specific about *why* children are completing a task or engaging with an activity. Imagine that a stranger entered the room and asked a pupil why he or she was doing the piece of work. Would the child reply blandly, 'Because teacher said'? Hopefully the child would have something more constructive to offer.

Separate statements from commands

Don't confuse children by making a statement when you should be giving a command. For example, *'Can you put your books away?'* is different in kind from *'Put your books away'* and is likely to be interpreted differently by the children. The first utterance is a question (implying a degree of choice); the second is an instruction (communicating insistence). Although the children gradually grow to understand that your question is, in reality, a requirement, it may be some time before vulnerable children grasp this fact, by which time you will have had to contend with numerous avoidable incursions of the rule. In maintaining order, avoid making general comments 'into the air'. For example, do not say: *'This class is making far too much noise. I've never heard anything like it!'* Instead, say to an individual or group of children: *'Please keep the noise down by speaking in a whisper and if you need to talk to someone on another table, go to them rather than shouting across the room'.* Try to model the behaviour you expect from the children: if you are bossy, fussy and loud, there is a strong likelihood that you will create a bossy, fussy and loud atmosphere in the classroom; if you are enthusiastic, level-headed and have a smiling disposition, these qualities will become widespread in the same way.

Use appropriate sanctions

Lively children – indeed, all children – need adult models of control and calmness, so use a relaxed tone of voice when it is necessary to exert discipline. Despite the temptation to do so, never shout unless you want the child to imitate you. If a punishment or sanction is necessary, it should be imposed as soon after the behaviour as possible. When the child deliberately continues to break a rule, it is perfectly acceptable to isolate him or her in a chair or a 'time-out' room. The time-out should last about one minute per year of the child's age; for example, an eight year old should be given up to eight minutes. The good practice that you employ for children with limited attention spans is relevant in organising learning for all children. If you can satisfy the needs and concerns of pupils who provide the greatest challenge, you can satisfy those of *any* child.

Extend your thinking

Genuine hyperactivity (as opposed to sheer naughtiness) is not a wilful act. You cannot eliminate the behaviour but you can assist in bringing it under reasonable control.

Children with physical limitations

All children deserve a good education, fair treatment and the chance to engage with every aspect of the curriculum in such a way that barriers to inclusion based on gender, intelligence and physical condition are swept away and there is genuine equal opportunity for all pupils. An important element of this inclusive provision includes the use of additional adult support in working one-to-one with physically disabled children, the availability of suitable resources and ease of access to rooms and spaces. In practice, the situation is rarely straightforward, owing to organisational problems (e.g. ramps, lifts and walkways may be difficult to maintain) and financial limitations (e.g. the purchase of expensive specialist equipment for the benefit of one child). Nevertheless, all adults working in school have a responsibility to make every effort to give each child a fair chance to succeed and enjoy learning.

Hearing impairment

We noted earlier in the chapter the fact that although most children's learning is enhanced through auditory means (i.e. from speaking and listening) there is always a small proportion who struggle due to a hearing impairment, which can sometimes go undetected. A temporary reduction in hearing capacity may result from a cold or virus or 'glue ear'; other children have a chronic (long-term) physical condition that necessitates the use of a hearing aid.

Many parents of seriously hearing-impaired children prefer that their children attend the local school rather than go to a school for deaf pupils, not least because they do not want their children to be thought of as 'odd' and partly because the children in the mainstream school will live locally, allowing for the growth of natural friendships that can be continued outside school. Some schools have a special unit for the deaf and hearing-impaired on the same site. The successful inclusion of deaf or hearing-impaired children in mainstream schools requires close cooperation between the family, audiologists and the school staff.

Teachers that work in mainstream schools usually have limited experience with hearing-impaired children, which is why cooperating with specialists is needed to provide the school staff with information and advice. Whatever the particular circumstances, the hearing-impaired child must not feel isolated from the other children because of the adverse psychological and social consequences. Classrooms should be organised to determine the best possible conditions for audibility. In some instances, an FM system or loop wire system can be installed to amplify the teacher's voice. Children with very poor hearing benefit from being able to look directly at the teacher, a point that is especially significant if the child is learning to lip-read. You should also be aware of any problem the child has with hearing aids during sports or on the playground.

Extend your thinking

When you look at that child, do you see a deaf child or a child who is deaf? Your perception will affect the way you behave and respond.

Children with other physical needs

There are a number of medical conditions associated with physical disability which can impact on pupils' mobility and learning, including serious conditions like spina bifida, cerebral palsy and muscular dystrophy and associated sensory impairments, neurological problems or learning difficulties. In the unlikely event of having such a child in your class, there will be additional adult support available, serviced through a 'statement' of special educational needs that will have been drawn up by teachers (probably the Special Educational Needs Co-ordinator, SENCO), a specialist from outside the school who can offer advice about the child's specific learning needs, and the parents.

The Department for Children, Schools and Families (DCSF) in England offers advice about providing a curriculum and teaching for children with special physical needs. *Visual impairment* is described in terms of difficulties ranging from partial sight through to total blindness, remembering that such pupils will represent the full range of ability. In practice, adaptations to the children's learning environment or the availability of specific learning materials in order to access the curriculum are normally required. For example, the child may need reading material with large print or equipment with labels that can be distinguished by touch, not sight. Pupils with *multi-sensory impairment*, as the name suggests, have a combination of visual and hearing difficulties, sometimes referred to as deaf/blind; however, some children may possess residual sight and/or hearing. If children have additional physical disabilities, assessment of their potential ability is problematic and requires specialist advice and support. As a trainee teacher you will not be expected to service the needs of children with extreme forms of disability but will be expected to play your part in ensuring that they receive the best possible treatment and education.

Extend your thinking

Disabled children don't want your sympathy but do appreciate your help and support. Why should they be doubly handicapped because their educational needs are being neglected?

Terminology check

Disability refers to the condition, whereas *handicap* refers to the effect of the situation on a child's ability to cope. In other words, a disabled child may or may not be handicapped by a situation, depending on the quality of the provision.

Common mistakes for beginner teachers

Trainee teachers make mistakes because they do not have a reservoir of previous experiences on which to draw and have not had time to develop an instinctive response to situations. The important thing is to avoid errors becoming embedded into your practice, such that they become systemic ('affecting every part of your work'). You will experience times when you are genuinely unsure about the best course of action; on other occasions you think that the way to proceed is obvious but it creates more problems than it solves. There may be moments when your inexperience leaves you floundering; your pulse rate rises and mild panic sets in. At such times be reassured that every teacher has endured such agonies of mind; with perseverance and thoughtful reflection, taking advice from mature practitioners, mixed with a healthy dose of determination, you will win through. It is invariably better to think ahead carefully than to rely on spontaneity alone, and the following descriptions of common errors of judgement offer a framework within which you can culti-vate such professional awareness:

ASSUMING THAT THE CHILDREN WILL ALL BE FASCINATED BY THE TOPIC

Instead, create interest by linking learning to previous experience and being interested in the topic yourself.

BEGINNING THE SESSION BY SPEAKING TOO FAST AND PROVIDING AN EXCESS OF INFORMATION

Instead, always begin gradually for the opening minute or so and build up the pace, introducing new knowledge in controlled portions rather than in a flood.

STARTING WITHOUT THE CHILDREN'S FULL ATTENTION

Instead, make sure that pupils are sitting upright and concentrating on your face.

TALKING TOO INTENSIVELY FOR TOO LONG

Instead, say a little, ask a thoughtful question, pause briefly; say a little more using a melodious rather than a flat or intrusive tone of voice.

USING A SURFEIT OF AUDITORY COMMUNICATION

Instead, use a variety of communication techniques, including simple visual aids.

USING TOO MANY VISUAL AIDS, SUPERFICIALLY

Instead, use a small number of aids thoroughly and squeeze all the learning out of each one that is possible by pointing out features, explaining links with other subject areas, asking speculative questions and, where appropriate, building a story around it.

FAILING TO INVOLVE THE TEACHING ASSISTANT

Instead, let her know what you are doing and, courteously, what you want her to do.

PLYING CHILDREN WITH NUMEROUS CLOSED QUESTIONS

Instead use a mixture of questions – open, closed and speculative – while remembering the principle that one decent question is worth five trivial ones.

STARING AROUND AT NO ONE IN PARTICULAR

Instead, look into the eyes (rather than 'through' the eyes) of different children, in the belief that eye contact is one of the most significant factors in fostering effective communication.

LOOKING TOWARDS AND AT THE SAME CHILDREN

Instead, rather than fixing your gaze only on children who express interest and respond eagerly or those who tend to be mischievous, include all the children.

ALLOWING CHILDREN TO MOVE POSITION WHILE YOU ARE ADDRESSING THE GROUP OR CLASS

Instead, unless you give them permission, children should remain in their starting positions unless there is an urgent health and safety reason for moving. Occasionally, children have a genuine need to visit the toilet or get a drink of water, but these occasions should be highly exceptional; once you allow one child to go, others will quickly want to follow.

FAILING TO SPOT THAT CHILDREN ARE BEING INATTENTIVE

Instead, don't become so fascinated with your own performance that you forget your audience; make sure that you are an active and alert sort of teacher who is 'outward' to pupils rather than 'inward' towards your lesson notes, electronic gadgetry and other immediate concerns.

RUSHING THROUGH THE LESSON WITHOUT PAUSING

Instead, write in deliberate pauses when you are preparing your lesson; make sure that pupils have opportunity to contribute; vary the nature of pupil involvement: a period of listening, of responding, of suggesting, of practical, of individual, and so on.

ALLOWING SPONTANEOUS AND UNSOLICITED INTERRUPTIONS

Instead, while you won't want to stifle enthusiasm, you must have a system for controlling excessive exuberance and (especially) cheeky behaviour.

SPEAKING LOUDER TO COMBAT NOISE, RESULTING IN A CACOPHONY OF SOUND AND STRAINED NERVES

Instead, use hand and eye signals where possible to bring children to order and, if necessary, stop speaking or decisively impose sanctions.

STANDING OR SITTING IN ONE SPOT FOR TOO LONG

Instead, unless it is unavoidable owing to a lack of space or the need to have access to static equipment, try to vary your position occasionally to re-focus the children, give yourself microseconds of relief from the intensity of teaching and allow your blood to circulate.

TRYING TO INGRATIATE YOURSELF WITH THE CHILDREN

Instead, be natural, do your job, persevere, be pleasant but not a push-over, keep the lesson moving, show that you care about the child as well as the work, encourage, enthuse, offer helpful advice and feedback and show your humanity.

FAILING TO INVOLVE CHILDREN IN THEIR OWN LEARNING

Instead, use every opportunity to explain what is going on and suggest ways that they might use their brains more profitably; after all, it is their learning, not yours.

DEPRIVING CHILDREN OF THE NECESSARY SKILLS AND UNDERSTANDING TO COMPLETE THE TASK OR ACTIVITY

Instead, make sure that you have spent sufficient time in checking that pupils have already grasped the basic knowledge required for the present work.

SETTING TASKS THAT CAN BE COMPLETED WITHOUT MUCH EFFORT

Instead, ensure that as well as all tasks and activities containing a straightforward element within the capability of every child, they should also contain progressively more difficult parts to challenge and extend the more capable pupils.

SETTING PURPOSELESS TASKS AND ACTIVITIES THAT ONLY SUBMISSIVE CHILDREN WILL DO WITHOUT PROTEST

Instead, explain the purpose of the work and where it fits with the overall sequence of learning; or simply admit that the activity is a means to an end (such as using old national test papers for revision purposes).

GIVING INADEQUATE TIME FOR COMPLETING WORK

Instead, allow a little more time than might be needed and incorporate an extension task for faster workers; it is pointless trying to force the pace and obliging pupils to terminate their work prematurely (which creates frustration) or rush to finish (which results in poor quality).

PROLONGING THE END PHASE

Instead, be brisk, point out praiseworthy features, indicate common errors, indicate the future direction and end positively.

SENDING THE CHILDREN FROM A DISORDERLY ROOM

Instead, make sure that you would not be ashamed of the state of the room were a prospective parent to walk in.

The list above – which could easily be added to – demonstrates the range of decisions that teachers have to make constantly if the session is to proceed successfully. Paying close attention to the way that you plan, conduct and evaluate lessons will ensure that even mistakes and miscalculations are not wasted, but contribute to your learning as well as to theirs.

Professional learning perspectives

Teacher authority

Willard Waller in his book, *Sociology of Teaching*, first published in 1932, comments as follows:

> The teacher must alternate his roles because he is trying to do inconsistent things with his pupils and he can bring them about only by rapid changes from one established pose to another. He is trying to maintain a definite dominance over young persons whose lives he presumes to regulate very completely [Role one] ... The solution is found in alternating this *authority* role with some other [Role two] which is not altogether inconsistent with it but which veils the authority so that hostility is no longer aroused. But the authority impression must be continually renewed, and there ensues a long series of rapid but not subtle changes of

role ... [Role two] says, 'But I am a human being and I try to be a good fellow. And you are all fine people and we have some good times together, don't we?' If the teacher tarries too long upon this *grace* note [Role two] he loses his authority by becoming one of the group. He must revert to Role number one [authority role] and say, with just a hint of warning and an implication of adult dignity in his voice, 'But I am the teacher'. All this occurs a hundred times a day in every school room and it marks the *rhythm of the teacher's movements of advancement and retreat* with reference to his pupils, the alternate expansion and contraction of his personality. [various extracts]

Developing trust

Dix (2007) advises new teachers as follows:

Model the behaviour that you want to see in your [pupils]. Arrive on time for your lessons, prepared for and enthusiastic about learning. Try not to show negative emotional reactions to the class when you are confronting undesirable behaviour but instead explain your frustrations as calmly and clearly as possible. You do not need to do this immediately ... Leave your purely emotional reactions for the privacy of home or friends, where you are not the role model.

Dix goes on to say,

Talk to them about their learning, how they feel when they attempt tasks that are challenging, unfamiliar or new. Then talk to them about your experience of learning. Demonstrate how you work around the frustration of not knowing the solution straight away.

He concludes,

By modelling and actively encouraging a calm and consistent approach to learning in the classroom you will start to develop an environment that is free from tension and fear. You will afford [pupils] the security and space they need to access higher order thinking skills and control their own behaviour. Trust will begin to develop. (extracts: pp. 10, 11)

Find out more by reading:

Ravet, J. (2007) *Are We Listening?* Stoke on Trent: Trentham.
Wright, D. (2005) *There's no Need to Shout!* Cheltenham: Nelson Thornes.

Chapter 7

Becoming a more skilful teacher

The content of Chapter 7 includes:

- the effect of different teaching and learning situations
- the importance of clarifying the lesson purpose(s)
- key points in organising a formal session
- ways to successfully conclude a formally planned lesson
- varying the tone and speed of your lesson format
- using questions as a strategy for learning
- the means and practice of explaining how, why, when and what
- the use of differentiation in lesson planning and teaching
- assessment, targets and records of pupil attainment.

Points to consider as you read this chapter:

1 How to modify your teaching to the prevailing conditions: time of day, size of space, number of pupils.
2 The importance of identifying and specifying the main lesson purposes without suppressing spontaneous opportunities for learning.
3 Approaches to planning, organising and managing a formal session.
4 The need to be clear about the purpose of using questions and ways to improve your technique.
5 How visual aids can improve your teaching if used appropriately.
6 The need to organise lessons so that each child can benefit.
7 The use of assessment to help you to enhance pupil learning.

Teaching and learning contexts

You cannot learn how to teach from a text book; not even this one! While the printed page and formal lectures offer insights and strategies, it is in the rough and tumble of classroom life that you sharpen your teaching abilities, make decisions about what is and is not appropriate for the children in your care, and learn to exercise judgement about your own and the pupils' behaviour. For this reason it is essential to gain experience in a variety of teaching situations, with pupils of different ages and abilities, larger and smaller groups of children, in closely confined and open areas (e.g. gymnasium, hall, games field), with and without additional adult assistance. The best teachers learn to discern the class 'mood' and adjust their teaching accordingly. Poorer teachers simply carry on regardless, seemingly oblivious to the prevailing circumstances. For instance, contrast the following sets of conditions that commonly occur in school and how they might impact upon your approach:

- first thing in the morning on a grey, bleak day in a chilly classroom
- immediately following an exciting drama presentation in the hall
- the afternoon preceding the half-term holiday
- during the winter when many of the children are coughing and wheezing
- a glorious summer's day towards the end of the year
- in the middle of the week of national testing.

If you taught precisely the same lesson to the same group of children on each of the occasions listed above, you would *have* to take account of the circumstances (sometimes referred to as the 'context') in order to promote the most effective learning and maintain interest. A lesson plan acts as a guide but cannot and should not dictate to you the emphasis to give to each aspect of the session, the precise amount of time to allocate to activities or the strategies you use to enforce discipline. The more experience you gain and the more you intelligently evaluate your role and purpose, the greater number of instant decisions you will get right. 'Thinking on your feet' is a necessary skill for every teacher at every level, but it requires perseverance and a willingness to evaluate your lessons carefully, reflecting *during* the situation and, afterwards, reflecting *about* the situation. Be careful not to confuse 'thinking on your feet' with 'on the hoof' instinctive responses borne of a need for classroom survival.

Extend your thinking

Successful teachers think ahead about what they *want* to happen, think on their feet about what *is* happening and think retrospectively about what *has* happened.

Despite the need to be alert to the social and academic features existing in each classroom (i.e. the specific abilities and attitudes that exist), there are some general operational principles in which it pays to invest time and effort. Once you have established the session framework, it allows you greater flexibility to experiment and modify what you do. Some inexperienced trainee teachers imagine that they can be innovative from the start, without establishing orderly routines and procedures. They soon discover their mistake.

Clarifying the lesson purpose

At the start of the session it is helpful to give the children a broad outline of what will happen and – prior to the task element – tell them about the *specific* aspects of the work that are important and about which you will be taking particular note. For example, if they are doing a piece of written work you may tell the children to do their best with spelling but that you are principally interested in looking at the range of ideas or sequence of steps they produce. On the other hand, you may be particularly interested in the way that they spell words, employ punctuation and shape the sentence structure but are less concerned about the content of the piece. You should not assume that children will instinctively know what you want or intend. Even if it is a problem-solving exercise in which you are more interested in the way that children work together than in the outcome of the investigation, you must explain the parameters of the activity (e.g. the need for discussion; correct use of equipment; time allocation).

A clear purpose should not be confused with having rigid ideas about what pupils are meant to learn to the exclusion of all else. In truth there are few sessions that are so specifically targeted towards a learning outcome that the objective can or should be singly pursued. There will always be a *core* learning objective or objectives and several *subsidiary* ones, but you must also stay alert to the *fortuitous* learning (sometimes referred to as 'serendipitous') that inevitably takes place at the same time. For instance, your core focus may be that the children should learn about combinations of particular letter sounds in phonics (e.g. a digraph/phoneme in which two letters make a single sound, such as 'ch'); the subsidiary learning may be the way in which the same combinations of letters sound different in other sets of words (e.g. comparing 'child' and 'chemist'); the fortuitous learning (which by definition cannot be predicted with certainty) may relate to how certain words are spelled; ideas about rhymes that contain 'ch' words; or questions that children raise about how to combine other letter shapes correctly. Bear in mind that mixed-ability classes require that you plan to accommodate pupils' different intellectual needs, so there will rarely be a singular plan of action, appropriate to every child.

In enquiry-based/investigative activities involving a large component of problem solving ('finding out') or in play-based activities, the amount of fortuitous learning may be substantial. Under such conditions it is important that children feel confident to raise points, ask questions and have opportunities to talk about other unpredicted forms of learning that may be emerging. Remember that learning is not like filling a petrol tank with diesel; it is more akin to blotting paper that absorbs moisture over a length of time. At the end of its contact with the moisture, the paper may be damp, wet or soaked. In the same way, a group of children, exposed to the same learning opportunities, will emerge with different understanding and knowledge, depending on their intellectual capacity, motivation and interest in the topic, and on your ability to focus their efforts. William Butler Yeats (Irish writer) once commented that education is not filling a bucket but lighting a fire. He was right!

Terminology check

Core learning objectives: the central planned purpose of a lesson.

Subsidiary learning objectives: other important planned learning during a lesson.

Fortuitous learning: unplanned discoveries that children make during the lesson.

Step by step through a formal session

There is no obligatory procedure for the way a session should be organised. While it is obvious that a formal maths lesson with (say) capable top juniors will differ markedly from (say) a play activity for four and five year olds or a PE session with lively eight year olds, there are key points relevant to every structured learning opportunity, as follows.

Settle the class so that children are actively hearing what you are saying

Children may appear to be listening but their minds can be elsewhere. A simple strategy such as saying 'please smile at me if you are ready' sets the scene for then insisting that the children sit up or stand still, repeat something that you have said and respond to your prompts. It is difficult to know how long to wait for children's attention but on balance the time you spend insisting in the early stages of meeting a class pays dividends in the long run. One scenario to avoid is a situation where you wait patiently for silence, while a disinterested group of pupils laugh and chatter among themselves without any intention of being compliant. Even worse is when the non-compliant group eventually jump to attention and pretend to be good then start talking again the moment you begin. Remain very calm and stern and make sure that they are left in no doubt that you intend to be obeyed. The practice of stressing the positive by making a general statement to thank all the children who are paying attention is fine, but avoid the wholly unnecessary and slightly pathetic habit of speaking to each child condescendingly: 'Well done, Sammy; well done, Andrew; well done, Ahmed', and so forth, while disobedience reigns elsewhere.

Introduce the lesson smartly

Although it is useful to speak more slowly and deliberately at first to allow children to tune in to your voice, it is best to get the session off to a brisk beginning and give pupils the strong impression that the lesson will be interesting. Make links with previous learning by referring to a key element, such as: 'Yesterday I was telling you a story about a real event that happened to some people who lived in our town' or asking a thoughtful question, such as: 'When we were struggling with division last time, put your hand up if you can remember how we finally worked out a way to divide the money fairly?' Once you have established the links, move on swiftly to explain what the session is about and state broadly what the children will be doing. Subsequently, you can offer a fuller explanation about tasks. Make the introduction serve its purpose and don't unduly extend it or allow the lesson to drag during this vital opening phase.

Strengthening practice

If you ask the children to 'come to order' and some of them continue to ignore what you say or half-heartedly comply, tell everyone to be *completely* still from the tops of their heads to the tips of their toes, then allow them to relax *gently*.

Maintain pace without rushing

Some inexperienced teachers are so keen to maintain pace that they confuse 'briskness' with 'haste'. *Pace* refers to lesson momentum – difficult to define but easy to detect for a tutor or teacher observing the session. Basically, it is rooted in purposeful learning, in which pupils and teachers are working in combination towards a specific goal. The ideal situation is where the session glides along and the children are so caught up in the wonder of learning that they don't have time or inclination to deviate from the task. Such pacing takes lots of practice and good organisation.

Explain expectations clearly

This step is so obvious yet it is easily overlooked in the desire to get the lesson moving. There are at least four ways to define 'expectations'. First, expectations expressed in terms of *learning objectives*, which give an indication about the sort of learning experience pupils should be immersed in. As we noted in Chapter 5, however, learning takes many forms and is not an easily definable 'entity' that can be neatly packaged and delivered seamlessly.

By clarifying your expectations about learning objectives you should not give the impression to pupils that you can predict precisely what they are going to learn, but rather to give them an indication of the core learning objective(s) and, perhaps, the subsidiary ones (see earlier). The second type of 'expectation' concerns the *logistics* of what follows: where children sit, how they work, with whom they liaise, what happens after completion and other organisational issues. Children ask more questions about these procedural aspects than about the work content. The third type concerns the *quality* of the work: what is important, what needs to be thought about most carefully, how the work is to be set out or recorded, what is essential and what is negotiable. Finally, 'expectation' must have regard to *behaviour*: fair play, tolerance and noise level. Though all four expectations must be addressed, the amount of time you allocate to each type will depend on the nature of the lesson. For example, a messy, practical session will probably require more attention to expectations as regards behaviour than would a 'heads-down' pencil-and-paper sort of session.

Extend your thinking

You must first have things straight in your *own* mind before you can transmit them clearly to the children.

Use a variety of questions

A question can serve many purposes. It can be used to gain children's attention, find out what some of them know, remind them of previous learning, make them think hard, create enthusiasm, act to counter over-exuberance or even generate controversy. The main point is that you must have a reason to ask the question and not ask questions for the sake of it. Although some questions arise spontaneously during the session, it is a useful strategy to have written down a few 'prompt' questions in advance, especially if you are inexperienced. Fisher (2005) warns against using too many questions that do not require pupils to think; instead, he advises that teachers should use fewer questions that demand more careful consideration. In fact there is a place for both 'closed and 'open' questions. *Closed* questions can be helpful to sharpen responses from dreamy children and offer an indication of knowledge mastery. *Open* questions allow children's minds to engage with content, draw in their own life experiences, think widely, innovate, speculate and predict. Regrettably, in the fast-moving world of the classroom, it is sometimes not possible to dwell on a narrow part of learning for too long. See p. 127 of this chapter for more information about questions and questioning.

Terminology check

A *closed* question is one in which there is a single correct answer or response.

An *open* question is one in which there are a variety of possible answers.

A *speculative* question is one in which pupils have to think about consequences.

Inform children about the subject content and the procedures

We noted above that it is important to be precise about what you expect or require; for example, how to set out the work on the page; materials to use in designing an item in design and technology (DT); procedures in a science experiment; how long is allowed on each play activity. However, it is equally important to ensure that pupils have the appropriate subject knowledge – or to know how to access it via book information or electronically – before proceeding with the set tasks. It is surprisingly easy for children to complete a task or activity successfully, yet never really engage with the content or have a firm grasp of the concepts involved. A typical example of this tentativeness is a pupil's completion of a set of computation problems without understanding the implications for employing the ideas and procedures in other contexts (such as shopping). Although all teachers need to be 'facilitators' – that is, to provide the conditions and climate for children to learn – it is equally necessary that you have a depth of knowledge and understanding of the subject matter and, especially when working with younger children, a firm grasp of learning theory.

Use resources effectively

The availability of basic resources such as a chair to sit on and a pencil to write with may not sound terribly important to you; however, for the child concerned it is a serious matter. Never assume that everything is in order: check or ask the assistant to do so, such that the session will not be interrupted by distressed or anxious children who are worried about the lack of simple but necessary items. More sophisticated equipment has to be kept under tighter control, especially when working with younger/dyspraxic ('clumsy') children who lack the dexterity or the necessary skills to use them correctly. An important element of your lesson is to ensure that pupils are competent in handling and caring for resources. Make sure, too, that the best resources are not allocated to the most insistent and confident children, while the timid ones hang back and meekly accept the remnants.

Terminology check

Dyspraxia is a childhood condition that affects motor skills and makes it hard for sufferers to focus on their work. It tends to make them clumsy and leads to problems in organising, spelling and writing. Their obsessive behaviour can result in a lack of friends.

Organise for learning

It is most probable that the host teacher has clear views about where children should sit and work. Some teachers are even strict about how, and where, children assemble 'on the carpet' and you must, of course, maintain that system. In addition, one of the fundamental decisions that you have to make about the task/activity phase is whether pupils work alone, in pairs or in small groups; you must also make it abundantly clear about the extent to which collaboration (helping one another) is allowed or encouraged, the time allowed to complete the task and the way to access the resources. If you don't tell the children what you are expecting in terms of the way they assist and support one another (or work independently) it is hardly surprising if they make an educated guess and sometimes get it wrong or ply you with questions of clarification.

Differentiate the work

The term 'differentiation' is used in three ways:

1   differentiation by *task*, in which children of differing abilities are given slightly different work of suitable challenge
2   differentiation by *outcome*, in which you judge the quality of the same piece of work with reference to a pupil's capability
3   differentiation by *expectation*, in which children attempt similar work but you have higher expectations of more able pupils.

Differentiation begins the moment the session begins and takes many guises. Thus, children with a low concentration span or impaired hearing or vision limitations may be asked to sit in a particular place to assist their learning. You may repeat instructions for the benefit of children who find it hard to absorb information first time. Your questions will take account of the fact that some children are less knowledgeable than others and probably include a few challenging ones for very able pupils.

The demands made by the tasks and activities will differ according to factors such as attention span, maturity, academic capability and experience of the subject area. In monitoring children's progress, your feedback will vary according to the misconceptions, misunderstandings or ability to progress further that each child displays. In drawing the session to a close you will take account of progress and development in framing your comments, allowing pupils to contribute and the amount of adult support deemed necessary in explaining results or outcomes. All the aforementioned elements have to be considered under 'differentiation'. See also assessment issues later in this chapter.

Terminology check

A *misunderstanding* denotes confusion borne of lack of clarity, which leads to a failure to understand or interpret something correctly.

A *misconception* means muddled thinking or inability to grasp the concept.

Monitor progress and intervene

There will be occasions when you want to stand back and allow the children to play, explore, grapple with problems and persevere. On other occasions you will impress upon pupils that they should use one another as sources of help and support, rather than immediately calling on an adult. Much of the time, however, your role will be in evaluating progress, noting occasions when children struggle, suggesting alternative approaches, insisting on specific action and clarifying confusions that arise in their minds. Monitoring and intervening is a hard-won skill but more manageable if you are clear about the principal learning intentions. It is easy to fall into the habit of intervening only when children are not concentrating or 'stuck' and to neglect opportunities to commend good behaviour, enthuse about progress and provide just enough information and guidance such that a child can make suitable decisions and gain confidence to go forward without feeling 'smothered' by excessive adult attention.

Offer appropriate feedback (formative assessment; assessment for learning, AFL)

An essential element of the monitoring and intervening agenda (see above) is to be keenly aware of the critical moments when pupils demonstrate through their words or actions that they have grasped a concept, developed a skill or gained some knowledge that assists their fuller understanding of a topic or theme. These assessment opportunities tend to present themselves through four pupil actions:

1   when they answer questions
2   when they complete a piece of work

3   when they explain something to an adult
4   when they share findings from a collaborative (team) exercise.

Good quality feedback based on 1 to 4 will commend, approve, suggest alternatives or re-direct their efforts. There is a considerable skill in offering advice and comment that assists but does not insist; prompts but does not push; commends but inspires greater effort.

Strengthening practice

Never assume that children will grasp something first time around. They need repetition, opportunities to talk, different perspectives and a chance to use their new knowledge in completing tasks, undertaking an activity or solving a problem.

Encourage and reward effort

Some children sail through school, enjoy work, do well and find favour with teachers. At the other extreme, a few children battle from the day they arrive until the day they leave. Most children have periods of progress and periods of consolidation: ups and downs, acceleration and regression, surges of understanding and periods of bewilderment. The majority of children will do their best to succeed by responding to your questions, completing the work and aiming high: they deserve regular encouragement and occasional lavish praise. However, a minority of children will be less enthusiastic, more reluctant to accommodate your wishes and weakly motivated; they will try hard occasionally, coast for much of the time and have moments of complete detachment from the work. You have the difficult task of deciding what sort of encouragement and verbal persuasion to use, such as (a) commending small steps of progress or (b) offering qualified praise or (c) issuing a warning. In plain language, you can say something like the following: (a) Well done, keep it up, or (b) Well done, but you will need to improve this and that area, or (c) If you don't do it then such-and-such will happen. Generally, it is better to err on the side of being upbeat about what children are doing but also to be explicit about what you expect from them. Decisions of this sort are far from easy: a child may not be attending to his or her work due to confusion about what is required or idleness or taking a few moments of mental respite or an inability to concentrate. You have to evaluate the situation in a few seconds and respond appropriately. A teacher's commendation is usually sufficient reward for most children; for the slouch or wilfully resistant pupil, however, it is necessary to use a combination of approval and warnings about consequences.

Extend your thinking

Do not tell the children about the reward *before* you have explained what you require them to do but *after* they have complied. In this way, what you give to them is truly a *reward* and not a *bribe*.

Cope with off-task behaviour

If you have taken the trouble to explain what children need to do and your expectations about the minimum standard required, the vast majority of children do their best to respond positively. Even so, there are bound to be momentary lapses and a few deliberate diversionary tactics, most often caused by one or more of the following five factors:

1   The child is naturally impulsive and distractible.
2   You have talked for too long.
3   The task is irrelevant, too difficult or confusing.
4   It is a particular time of the day (such as close to lunch) or an unusual event (such as an important visitor).
5   Two or more pupils are 'working off each other' to generate fun and frolics rather than effort and enterprise.

The important thing is to be keenly aware of these factors and take appropriate action to prevent or minimise them taking place, rather than waiting for the misbehaviour and having to disrupt the lesson by telling off children, writing their names on the board or whatever remedial action is applicable.

Bring things to a halt

The task/activity phase allows opportunity for pupils to practise skills, reinforce their present knowledge, play with ideas, rehearse what has gone before or apply their knowledge. It is a source of frustration for many children that teachers do not give them sufficient time to complete the set work, leaving them feeling unfulfilled and disappointed. While there is a limited period that children can concentrate, it is better to err on giving them more rather than less time, particularly in an enquiry-based lesson (finding out/exploring a problem) or one in which teamwork plays an important part. It is absurd to spend a lot of effort in organising an activity and then curtailing it before pupils can achieve anything of value and telling them to 'pack away' in advance of the lesson review. You may as well have told them the answers in the first place and spent the time doing more profitable things! In practical sessions particularly, it is essential to give pupils a warning some ten, five and one minute before they have to complete what they are doing. Always leave a further minute or two of flexibility to allow for slower workers and a few children so desperate to finish what they are doing that they are prepared to face your anger rather than conclude prematurely. Be patient with such eager types; if only all children were so keen to learn!

Extend your thinking

It is an indication of a successful lesson when children complain about having to finish and pack away.

Dismiss the class

Experienced teachers make dismissal look so easy; for trainee teachers, however, it is essential to be clear about the conditions under which you are willing to release children from the session. For instance, you may decide that pupils can go once they have handed in their work and tidied their places; on the other hand, you may insist that no one leaves until everyone has cleared away to your satisfaction; yet again, you may dismiss a table at a time, depending on (say) if the children are sitting up straight and quiet. One way and another you must control the dismissal and not be caught out by a general exodus, accompanied by noise and confusion, as misbehaviour is far more likely under such conditions, with all the embarrassment and possible humiliation for you that follows in trying to retrieve the situation. Don't neglect this end phase in your desire to bring about rapid lesson closure and get the children out of the room (see also p. 124).

Assess the completed task

Once the session is over you will want to evaluate the quality of children's work and their progress (a process often referred to as 'assessment of learning', AOL). During the lesson you will have carried out continuous assessment *for* learning (AFL) but now you are concentrating on assessment *of* learning, which can take many forms depending on the task of activity they were undertaking: written task, speaking and listening, creating something visual, etc. Your assessment will also need to take into account three additional factors:

1   whether children worked singly, in pairs or in groups
2   the amount of adult support that was offered in completing the task/doing the activity
3   the difficulty and demands of the work.

It is sometimes helpful if your feedback is written, though if you intend principally to encourage rather than assess, the use of a simple visual indicator is sufficient (sticker, smiley face, star, etc.). If the task is for a special purpose, in as much as you have deliberately established it to evaluate pupil progress in a specific area, more detailed feedback from the assessment is required, so build that process into your planning.

Strengthening practice

Use assessment 'of learning' as a source of information to inform plans 'for learning'.

Concluding the session

We noted earlier that concluding the lesson requires as much attention and careful consideration as any other aspect of your work as a teacher and its smooth operation is essential to complete a successful session. The lesson conclusion serves at least four purposes:

1   *To finish tasks or leave them at a suitable point for further development at a later time.* It is often the case that the set tasks do not fit neatly into the time allocated for the session and need to be left at a suitable point such that the children can continue or complete the work in the near future. If you neglect to develop a theme or topic when the children's learning is incomplete – supplementing with further examples or revising what has been done – the effort that has been so far expended will be of limited value.

2   *To draw together the threads of learning.* Children should be encouraged to understand their own learning, see the purpose of the present work and grasp its implications in a wider context. The concluding minutes of the session can be used constructively to talk about such issues, share findings, celebrate successes and get disappointments and setbacks into perspective by emphasising that a lack of success is not necessarily a failure. The only real failure is an unwillingness to try. Lack of success in achieving the stated goal may be due to a number of factors: insufficient time to complete the activity; the task was too hard or inappropriate; uncertainty about what was required; working with an unsuitable partner; conceptual confusion or misunderstanding about a key element of the work. It is the last point that is most relevant here. If you can use the concluding moments of the session to identify and (perhaps) rectify or begin to rectify the confusion, the time will have been well spent.

3   *To leave the room in good order.* If you are a trainee teacher using someone else's room or work area, it is discourteous to conclude the session without

spending time ensuring that items are replaced, equipment is put away and finished work is stored appropriately. If the lesson is completed in the sense that the subject matter does not require further attention, the product of the session must be handed in for marking or placed in an easily retrievable place. If the lesson is incomplete (see point 1 above) there are decisions to make about the practicalities of storing the work. Separate sheets of paper are easy to crease, so if the work is a final version, great care must be taken in storing it; draft paper versions (with names) can normally be placed in a collection tray. If the work is generated through a computer, it may pay to print it off later when the situation is less pressurised. If delicate 3D items or paintings are involved, storage is obviously more problematic and you must think carefully in advance about where they should go. The simple expedient of children writing their names on the product or a label to identify it is elementary but surprisingly easy to forget.

4   *To look ahead ('next steps').* It is important to review the principal, subsidiary and fortuitous learning that have taken place with the children but also to think about the next steps in the lesson sequence and where the present learning touches other areas, both in the subject area under consideration and, ideally, the links with other parts of the curriculum. The more accurately you can determine the extent of children's learning in the immediate past (AOL), the better equipped you will be to plan effectively for the future.

Extend your thinking

The concluding phase is equivalent to rush-hour traffic. Make sure that you give it a lot of thought in advance and stay alert until the road is clear.

Twelve steps to facilitate a successful lesson

1   Know what you are doing and let the children know what they are doing.
2   Spend a little time finding out what the children already know.
3   Introduce the lesson enthusiastically, linking it with previous work.
4   Use a few open-ended questions to encourage pupil thinking.
5   Describe the tasks, their relevance and your expectations.
6   Clarify whether pupils have to work in silence or can speak to their classmates.
7   Explain whether the task is an individual or a collaborative one (in pairs or small groups).
8   Get involved with their learning: monitor, intervene and redirect their efforts.
9   Stand back from time to time, noting how children are concentrating and coping.

10 Give a finishing time warning and clarify what happens to the work on its completion.

11 Summarise what has been learnt and what remains to be learnt.

12 Briefly celebrate achievement and mention what happens next.

Varying the tone and speed of delivery

Some people have mellifluous voices; you could listen to them all day. At the other extreme, some people have harsh voices that grate on the eardrum. It is worth persevering to train your voice to become more of the smooth and less of the scratchy by regularly using a number of simple techniques. First, practise breathing steadily when you are standing in a relaxed pose, consciously channelling the air deep into your lungs. Second, breathe in slowly and then release the air gradually through the mouth, occasionally stopping the flow for a second or two, before continuing with the same breath. Third, let your speaking voice 'bounce' out in a single breath, saying dum-diddy-dum (or similar) up and down the scale, all the time keeping your back relaxed and shoulders comfortably still.

Do not make the mistake of confusing a clear voice with a strident one. If you feel your voice working its way up your throat and into your mouth (often accompanied by dryness) make an effort to ease it back towards your lungs and use your lips and tongue to shape the sound and not to produce it. Humming or singing gently can also assist voice production. Perhaps, though, the most effective way to improve voice quality is to record yourself speaking. It will make you grimace initially but give firm clues about areas for improvement, notably diction, pace of speech and clarity of message.

Anxiety can result in an over-rapid delivery and hurried explanations that cause confusion and irritation for children, who are struggling to interpret what you are saying. Always allow a little time for pupils to adjust to your voice by speaking accurately and more slowly than normal during the first moments of addressing them. Remember, too, that younger children often appear to be listening when they are merely looking in your direction. By contrast, older children can be listening to you when they appear to be uninterested. Techniques to aid communication include using a 'say after me' technique, whereby the children repeat the phrase that you have spoken, keeping the phrases simple but relevant to the lesson. As pupils repeat what you have said, they not only tune in to your voice but the act of engagement with the content obliges them to concentrate and activates their minds.

When *reading in unison* with the group or class it is important to speak at about half the speed that you imagine necessary. Never hesitate to read through an important piece of text a second time if necessary and in doing so, vary your voice and delivery occasionally by using a hushed tone, missing out key words or emphasising particular categories of word by speaking louder or varying the pitch. See below for a summary of strategies when reading in unison.

In common with speech in other forums, reduce the rate at which you speak if you want to emphasise a point or suddenly speed up for a few seconds if you want to stir sluggish brains.

Strategies when reading in unison

- Begin by speaking very slowly.
- Pause at the end of every second sentence.
- Get different sets of children to read in turn.
- Read dramatically, using different voices.
- Slow down towards the end of the piece.
- Sing out the words.

Extend your thinking

In every session, teachers have to fulfil two overlapping roles: (a) the role of 'sage on the stage', directing from the front and leading the learning in a carefully pre-determined route; (b) the role of 'guide from the side', giving children freedom to select and make choices, while providing resources and offering suggestions about direction and priorities.

Extending learning through use of questions

One way in which every teacher tries to engage pupil interest is by asking questions; unfortunately, too many question-and-answer sessions are little more than a guessing game disguised as learning. It is not always appropriate to ask a question and it may be better to think of imaginative ways to *tell* the children memorably instead, employing visual aids where appropriate. On the other hand, asking questions serves a valuable purpose in harnessing attention and getting children to think and share ideas. Questioning also offers insights into children's existing knowledge and understanding, though this element has limitations, as it is difficult to gauge whole group or class attainment based on a few selected responses.

One of the guiding principles about asking questions is to make all of them interesting and some of them thought provoking. For instance, contrast these questions about the same issue:

- What is the answer if you add together two metres and one metre?
- What would happen if a man who is two metres tall woke up tomorrow morning one metre taller than he is today?

The first question is plain, with a single correct answer that children will or will not be able to work out. The second question first requires that children stop and think, use their imaginations, conceptualise the problem, work out its meaning, translate it into a number bond and produce the correct mathematical answer, before responding to the heart of the question, namely, predicting what would *happen*. It is quite likely that some young children will first offer a response based on their imaginations:

He won't fit on the bed.
His feet will stick out of the window.
His clothes will tear open.

They may probe his emotional condition:

He would be very scared.
He'd wonder what was happening.
His friends would run away.

The mathematical solution to this elementary problem does not demand much intellect but the implications for engaging pupil interest and deepening their learning are profound. For instance, you may extend their thinking by asking questions such as:

How tall would he be if he grew by only half a metre?
Say he shrunk by half a metre each day: how long would it take before he was all gone?
Say he grew by half a metre every day, how long would it be before he reached the chimney if the house is 5 metres high?

And with older or more able pupils, you could push the boundaries of their thinking even further. For example:

If he kept growing for a week at the same rate, about how long would it take him to walk to the shop, 200 metres away? (Note the conceptual complexity in this mathematical operation.)

Or you could ask a question involving a value judgement, such as:

Would it be fair to let him play basketball for the local team?

Obviously, these challenging questions would require time for pupils to work out a solution (perhaps in pairs). There are three factors to be considered in deciding how far to push the extent and nature of questioning and extend the boundaries of learning:

1   *The principal learning intentions for the session.* You cannot afford to stray too far from the lesson aims or you might never get back on track.
2   *The age and ability of the children.* Able and older pupils will generally be capable of exploring difficult concepts more readily than younger, less able

pupils. On the other hand, the children may surprise you by the extent to which they can grasp quite advanced and abstract ideas once they are placed within a familiar context.

3   *The amount of time available.* Speculating, exploring and investigating ideas and concepts, with high pupil involvement, take more time than a didactic ('tell them') approach or narrowly focused learning. In a world of time-tables and targets, your teaching may have to be less creative than you would ideally prefer it to be.

Strengthening practice

Ask a TA or fellow-student or the class teacher to monitor which children you choose to answer questions over a couple of sessions and see what the results tell you about your choices.

Terminology check

Concrete learning: pupils absorb information through direct ('hands-on') experience, by doing, acting, sensing and feeling.

Abstract learning: children absorb information through analysis, observation and thinking, but may also choose to employ direct experience.

Building on pupils' answers

If a pupil answers well, commend the child and repeat the answer for the rest of the class. Although *you* hear the correct answer, there is a good chance that half the class has not heard it in the sense of absorbing the information and its implications, either because they physically did not hear or they were not paying attention or they did not understand. For example, imagine that you ask some infant children to give you different meanings for the word 'bow' as you hold up the word written on a card (but refrain from speaking the word aloud). Their responses might include what you do when you meet the queen and the sound a dog makes. Another pupil might volunteer that 'bow' forms part of the word 'rainbow' and, to reinforce learning, you could respond by saying the following:

*   Well done, Alison! Yes, the word 'bow' is found in rainbow.
*   We can see a rainbow in the sky after rain followed by sunshine.
*   Hands up anyone who has seen two rainbows in the sky at the same time.
*   Let's all spell the word 'rainbow' by saying the letters together.
*   Draw an arc in the air with your finger if you know the colours of the rainbow.

Alternatively, you could turn nearly all the steps in the sequence into questions:

- When does a rainbow appear in the sky?
- Who can spell 'rainbow'?
- What are the colours of the rainbow, in order?

At first sight the above sequence may seem unnecessarily complicated, but reinforcing an answer in this way only takes a short time and ensures that every child is immersed in that tiny unit of learning.

Extend your thinking

If you can make your pupils think deeply, speak purposefully and ask questions that interest them, you have gone a long way towards establishing a meaningful learning environment.

Explaining how, why, when and what

We have noted elsewhere the fact that one essential skill you need to develop is the ability to explain things clearly, as numerous misunderstandings and instances of unsettled pupil behaviour are caused by failings in this area. Explanations can be categorised under four headings:

1   Explaining how.
2   Explaining why.
3   Explaining when.
4   Explaining what.

Of the four types, explaining *how* is by far the most commonly used. Thus: how to go about the task; how to use equipment; how to work something out; how to spell a word; how to make a correct decision, and so on. It is not only important to tell pupils how but also to encourage them to 'tell you back' what you have said, for although children may appear to understand, they have not necessarily grasped the detail.

Explaining *why* is used to justify a decision or value position or as a form of reassurance and may arise from children asking for an explanation about why such and such a decision was made or a particular action is necessary. It is best to answer children's questions honestly but unapologetically. Be as open as possible – bearing in mind pupil age and maturity – while acknowledging areas of uncertainty and, in the area of value judgements, differing opinions.

Explaining *when* relates to small but important matters such as how long children have got to complete a piece of work, moving on to the next learning phase or taking their turn to use resources. Children become uneasy if they are concerned about time factors; clarifying the position allows them to concentrate on their work without worrying unduly about whether they will complete the task in the time allowed.

Explaining *what* is a more complex form of explanation that explores concepts and issues in such a way that a child can better understand how areas of knowledge inter-relate. For instance, to investigate what results from different conditions in science or technology; to search for patterns in mathematics; to analyse or synthesise text to draw out richer meanings; to share ideas about an author's intentions.

You may note from the above model that the four types are not independent and overlap; nevertheless, it pays to work on improving the quality of your explanations at a whole class and individual level. Locating explanations in real-life examples, using story lines where possible and utilising visual aids, further enhances understanding. For example: *'Put your hand up if you have ever gone to play in the park and nearly been knocked on the head by a swing...'* as a prompt to introduce an aspect of health and safety or of movement in science. A story line such as, *'Imagine you were king or queen or prime minister for a day. I wonder what laws you would pass?'* can be a means of probing issues relating to power, fairness and respect for others as an element of the Citizenship curriculum (see Invernizzi and Williams, 2007).

Strengthening practice

To stimulate discussion, try this question with younger children: *What would happen if nothing ever died?* With older pupils ask: *Which is better? To be rich and live until you are 40 or poor and live to be 100?*

Terminology check

Citizenship education (primary phase) is often delivered alongside PSHE (personal, social and health education) with an emphasis on the individual, their friends and their community.

Using aids to support teaching

Aids can enhance pupil learning by providing visual prompts, clues, stimuli and summaries of key facts or issues. There are two main ways to categorise aids: (a) into electronic and non-electronic, (b) into those that are used just once and those that can be used repeatedly. From a time management point of view it is sensible to place more effort into producing aids that can be re-used than those that have only a once-only use, though it is unwise to spend too long on a first version in case it proves to be unsuitable. It is tempting to design something impressive for a single lesson, but far better to keep such materials plain and simple initially and make improvements after using them in your teaching.

Although we often assume that the most effective aids are computer-related, there are many simple ways to enhance children's understanding and heighten their interest without recourse to technology. For instance, if you need to point to a word, why not have a decorated 'pointing stick'? You can even give it a name, such as Poppy Pointer or Happy Harry. Again, paper copies of pictures and photographs may not have the same visual impact as a blown-up version on screen, but they can be handled, scrutinised and mounted as part of a tableau or in displays, together with questions and statements to prompt pupil thinking and raise excitement. Of course electronic aids are immensely useful and there are many computerised systems available by means of which lesson content can be loaded in advance, diagrams and charts can be thrown onto the screen to aid visibility, and samples of work can be digitally photographed and shared with children at an appropriate point in the lesson. The decision that you have to make is the extent to which the benefits of employing these strategies outweigh the time and effort they take to organise and manage. It is not worth spending an excessive amount of time on the aids at the expense of the other elements of teaching. On the other hand, if you see that your preparation of visual aids (electronic or otherwise) is having a positive effect on children's attitude towards learning and grasp of the topic, you can feel confident that the time expenditure is justified.

Strengthening practice

Always trial your visual aids before spending a lot of time preparing sophisticated versions for more permanent use.

Differentiation

As noted earlier, differentiation is a rather clumsy term used to describe the way in which a lesson is organised and managed, such that children of different abilities are catered for in how the curriculum is presented and taught. In recent years the concept of differentiation has been somewhat superseded by the notion of 'personalisation', whereby individual needs are assessed and targeted provision made to remedy the pupil's perceived knowledge weaknesses, especially in literacy and mathematics (see Chapter 5).

Differentiation has been traditionally thought of with respect to distinguishing the types of tasks with which children engage: the less competent group A deal with easier task A, the more capable group B have harder task B to complete, and so on. A variation on this theme is to give the whole group or class the same set of tasks but to grade the activities in order of difficulty, commencing with simpler ones and gradually increasing the conceptual demands. The benefit of grading is twofold: first, it avoids publicly dividing children on the basis of ability, thus helping to preserve the fragile confidence of less capable pupils; second, it allows children to engage with the work until they reach their optimum level of competence and is therefore self-regulating.

Differentiation can also be considered from the perspective of the *time* in which tasks are completed, posited on the inevitable fact that children work at different speeds. Early finishers require extension tasks appropriate to their ability to avoid them 'sitting around' or aimlessly filling their time as they wait for their slower classmates to finish. However, although speed of work is often an indicator of competence, it is not necessarily the case that the first pupil to complete a task has the firmest grasp of the concepts involved. Some children are sprinters and others are middle-distance runners; a few are tortoises. It may also be chastening for you to realise that your carefully prepared task may require only minimal concentration from pupils and can be achieved without undue effort. Older children love to compete with their friends to see who can finish first, so you need to check that the quality of work is of an acceptable standard. If the same children keep finishing early it is a clear sign that one or both of two things applies: either the work is insufficiently demanding or they are not taking it seriously enough and doing the bare minimum that they can get away with to satisfy you.

Extend your thinking

Never underestimate what a child can achieve with your advice, support, guidance and encouragement.

Assessment, targets and records

Learning takes a variety of forms such that, for instance, it is possible to do well in tests and examinations, yet still lack social skills, discernment and self-discipline. Similarly, the pupil who writes correctly, using accurate grammar and spelling, may or may not produce imaginative pieces. By contrast, the child who is spilling over with ideas and suggestions may be unable (or unwilling) to concentrate on a task and see it through to completion. In modern school life, pupils have to be well-rounded learners in the sense that they can deal with the 'business end' of education by having a good grasp of reading, writing and mathematics such that they can succeed in local and national tests, but also retain their enthusiasm, spontaneity, willingness to try new ideas and team spirit.

Generally, your role during the work/activity phase is orientated towards assessment 'for' learning (AFL) – that is, you provide assistance and intervene regularly so that the children can improve what they are doing and achieve their best standard of work. AFL strategies involve extensive feedback about work quality, answering pupils' questions, showing them how to accomplish outcomes more effectively or ways to improve their skills, focusing their attention on priorities and broadening their horizons by speculating and prompting deeper thinking through the use of stimulating questions. If the lesson is orientated more strongly towards an assessment 'of' learning (AOL) you remain more detached from the situation and only clarify what must *be* done, rather than *how* to do it.

Sometimes assessment of learning takes the form of a test that is designed to throw light on specific aspects of pupils' knowledge and understanding; sometimes the assessment is more broadly based to ascertain which particular elements of a theme or topic are causing problems. However, these two assessment categories (AFL and AOL) overlap in various ways; in fact, it is impossible to offer feedback about learning (AFL) without at the same time making an on-the-spot assessment of the child's present understanding (AOL). Similarly, it would be foolish to conduct an AOL and not to take account of the results when planning future lessons. There are, therefore, some aspects of assessment that overlap the AFL and AOL agendas, which I shall refer to as 'assessment of and for learning' (AOFL). It is useful to constantly ask yourself which assessment mode you are operating in and its relevance for children's learning and your teaching. The following guide will help you to identify the assessment mode in which you are operating.

Assessment FOR learning (AFL)

- You set tasks or ask work-related questions.
- You find out what children know, understand and can explain.
- You are sensitive to individual needs and progress.
- You closely monitor pupil behaviour, attitude and concentration.
- You make judgements about the things children say and do.
- You weigh pupil attainment against your principal and subsidiary learning objectives.

Assessment OF and FOR learning (AOFL)

- You offer children directions about appropriate ways to deal with a task or understand a problem or issue.
- You mark work with the child present.
- You summarise for the group or whole class key learning points or explore misconceptions.
- You affirm that pupils are working well and succeeding.
- You discuss the implications for learning of your feedback comment or the award of a particular mark or grade.

Assessment OF learning (AOL)

- You provide a comment, mark or grade to indicate the level of achievement against previously established criteria.
- You record a mark or grade on pupils' work and/or in your own records.
- Your mark or grade is shared with the pupil or colleague or parent/carer.
- You take account of assessment information in planning future lessons.

If you are an inexperienced teacher dealing with a large group or the whole class it is extremely useful to have another person observing the children, as it is difficult to teach and assess pupil responses and present achievements at anything other than a superficial level. Fellow students, classroom assistants and even the class teacher can provide invaluable service in this regard but you will need to be clear with them about precisely what you want them to look for.

Assessment permeates every aspect of a teacher's work, from the regular technique of asking questions to ascertain pupil knowledge, through to sophisticated analyses of children's writing and reading. As a result of the emphasis on assessment, the importance of setting targets for pupil learning and recording data has assumed great significance, while bearing in mind that many elements of learning are 'in transition' and not easily quantifiable ('given a number'). A summary of strategies, factors guiding intervention, evidence used to set targets and limitations of records are listed below.

Assessment strategies to monitor pupil progress

- direct observation about the pupil's level of engagement with the work, reliance on classmates, speed of task completion
- asking a range of questions: closed questions to assess knowledge and memory; open questions to assess thinking skills and the ability to express ideas
- putting children in pairs to discuss issues or problems and listening as they summarise findings
- taking in work and evaluating its quality against criteria
- encouraging children to tell you what they have done and why
- using self-assessment.

Factors guiding intervention

- the child's previous history of coping with similar work demands
- whether children are working alone or collaboratively
- whether a child appears distressed, bored or distracted
- your expectations about quality of work and behaviour
- the extent to which a child requests adult help
- your knowledge of the child as a person
- the noise level.

Evidence used to set pupils' targets for learning

- the child's progress compared with others
- identifying specific areas of need and concern
- the areas in which a child requests additional support
- the results of formal tests
- the identification of misconceptions
- needing to reach agreed curriculum goals
- your perceptions of a child's capability to achieve more.

Strengthening practice

Take account of the following limitations in recording pupil achievements:

- Records cannot convey the nature of the learning climate.
- Records cannot describe the child's disposition at the time the work was done.
- Records say nothing about the teacher's role in assisting pupil attainment.
- Children attain things that are not easily measured or recorded.

Extend your thinking

Targets are valuable servants but ruthless masters.

Professional learning perspectives

Using classroom observation

There has been a considerable emphasis in recent years on the importance of assessing children's progress in learning. However, in doing so we do well to note the warning given by the noted educationist, Christian Schiller, in his classic book, *Christian Schiller: in his own words* (1979):

> To assess attainment it must be observed in the round. Such observation is not easy. The observer has not only to use keenly his eyes and ears but also to know where to direct them. He has not only to see and hear the shape of an event but also to perceive its quality. Observation, in this sense, is subjective, and its value depends on the judgement as well as the skill of the observer. Observation is sometimes used in the limited sense of noting the

score on a standard scale: it will be convenient to call this 'measurement'. … [however] … Observation alone can show the way a child is living and growing and can note the quality of his behaviour. (p. 3)

Successful assessment practice

Hall (2007) summarises the challenge for the beginner teacher with regard to successful assessment practice as follows:

> The challenge for the beginner teacher, having recognised the significance of the learner's role in assessment and the integral nature of assessment and learning, is to assess children in a variety of ways, taking account of a range of evidence and a range of learning contexts. The best way to meet this challenge is to use good learning tasks as sources of evidence of learners' success and difficulty, to see the learner's thinking as central to the assessment process and to involve learners in the assessment process. (p. 203)

Find out more by reading

Clarke, S. (2008) *Formative Assessment in Action: Weaving the Elements Together*, London: Hodder Arnold.

Hall, K. (2007) 'Assessing children's learning', in Moyles, J. (ed.) *Beginning Teaching, Beginning Learning in Primary Education*, Maidenhead: Open University Press.

Johnston, J., Halocha, J. and Chater, M. (2007) *Developing Teaching Skills in the Primary School*, Maidstone: Open University Press.

Part 3

Trainee teachers on school placement

Chapter 8

Challenges and opportunities on school placement

The content of Chapter 8 includes:

- how your attitude to the placement makes a difference to your progress
- ways of handling emotions
- key issues and challenges on placement
- how to turn situations to your advantage
- dilemmas in teaching: case studies of trainee teachers' experiences.

Points to consider as you read this chapter:

1 Ways in which you can constructively use your enthusiasm for teaching.
2 The need for awareness about the challenges and opportunities on placement.
3 The importance of adopting a positive approach to life in school.
4 Using targeted strategies to resolve specific situations.

Introduction

Regardless of how hard you work and how sincere your level of commitment, time spent on placement in school is always going to prove challenging as well as rewarding. Every training course involves time spent in actively engaging with pupils and teachers in an educational setting (school, college, nursery, etc.) and provides opportunities for you to hone your teaching skills and learn about the various teacher roles in a progressive way, supported by a tutor and the host staff of the school. It is more than likely that you will always be in a supportive environment where you feel comfortable and able to make progress without being fearful that genuine errors will count against you. Sometimes your placements will vary; most of them will be fine, one or more of them may not be to your liking. That's life! You simply have to stay positive, refuse to countenance long-term failure but accept that short-term setbacks are inevitable. It is worth noting, however, that trainees with an upbeat approach to life generally have a higher percentage of suitable placement schools than those trainees with a downbeat approach to life. This apparent 'luck' is due to the fact that some trainees *perceive* their placement as offering advantages, rather than it necessarily being that way. In other words, two trainees can be in the same school situation: one views it positively; the other adopts a negative stance. Which trainee teacher do you imagine is more likely to get the most benefit from the experience?

It is essential to learn quickly the rituals, routines and procedures that characterise the school and classroom to which you are attached during a placement. Areas of school life and routines to which you should be alert include the following ...

- normal staff times of arrival and leaving
- registering pupils present and absent
- storage and access to 'lunch boxes'
- availability of fruit and refreshments for children
- the responsibilities of different teachers
- staff room practices and procedures
- playground duties
- the role of teaching assistants
- getting pupils to and from assembly
- systems for rewards and sanctions
- the purpose of different staff meetings
- accessing consumable resources, books and equipment
- pupil fitness programmes
- reading systems and records
- extra-curricular opportunities
- procedures when a child is injured.

Early in the placement you may have relatively little opportunity to teach but you can usefully spend the time learning about the elements of school life listed above. As you orientate to the situation you will slowly become aware of other 'hidden' features that characterise the day-to-day life. You must learn these small but significant idiosyncrasies if you are to be integrated into the school's social fabric. For instance, it may be the norm for teachers to smile when they pass in the corridor and say something like, 'How is it going?' or share chocolate biscuits with neighbouring colleagues or meet together on a Friday lunchtime. On the other hand, certain behaviour may be unacceptable; for example, leaving an outdoor coat in the staff room or talking about politics. Sometimes there are gender-specific 'unspoken' rules, such as female teachers not wearing high heels or male teachers not wearing denim trousers.

Dress codes (explicit or unstated) are more significant in some schools than in others; it is worth making discrete enquiries.

Emotions associated with school placement

To make the best use of your time in school you need to do a lot of hard thinking *before* you begin and also *during* the placement. Progressing as a teacher is not a hit and miss affair; it requires diligent academic study, careful application of ideas and a willingness to sacrifice your security and venture into new areas of experience, both in terms of the subject areas you teach and the range of responsibilities you undertake. It is daunting to teach something for the first time or handle a full class when you have been used to just a single group, but ultimately far more fulfilling and, of course, ultimately necessary if you are to progress beyond 'assistant teacher' to 'main teacher'.

If you are experiencing some anxiety or excited anticipation about your time in school, be assured that you are in good company! All trainee teachers have a mixture of emotions before the event; on the one hand they are eager to teach and be part of the school community, on the other hand they are nervous about being overwhelmed by the demands of the task. For instance, Prudence was full of excitement on the eve of her placement:

> Final school experience had arrived. Eleven weeks of placement at a large primary school was to be my destination. My emotions were running high. This was it! Time to prove myself. A teacher is what I had always wanted to be and it was nearly within my reach.

Anticipatory emotions are often characterised by a conglomerate of questions and feelings in the minds of trainees. Gemma described her feelings as follows:

> As school placement approaches you are filled with a mixture of emotions. Questions spin around in your head: Where will I be placed? What age will the children be? What will the school be like? Will it be anything like last time? This fear of the unknown and uncertainty generates feelings of excitement and anxiety.

Elspeth was honest about the mixture of emotions she felt and describes her time in school as an 'emotional journey':

> There are always mixed feelings initially because no matter how many teaching experiences you have, each one always feels like your first. From day one you begin an emotional journey of excitement as well as apprehension in terms of whether or not you will fit into the school and be able to become an active member within it.

You will note that emotions are particularly strong prior to the placement and it is possible to allow your imagination to conjure up all sorts of questions into your mind:

- Are the children well behaved or troublesome?
- Is the class teacher kind, bright and welcoming or uninspiring and prone to finding fault?
- Is the classroom large and airy, with adequate workspace and good resources or cramped and stale, with inadequate equipment?
- Are the other teachers and assistants cheerful and informal or brisk and businesslike?
- At what time am I expected to arrive on the first day and subsequently?
- How long am I expected to stay after school?
- Whereabouts in the classroom can I keep my possessions and resources for teaching?
- How many other trainee teachers will be there at the same time?
- Does the school have a hall and outdoor spaces for games?
- Do I have to attend all staff meetings?

Answers to most of these questions are found within the first day or two of starting, so it is not worth expending too much anxious energy in pondering them. More important questions relate to the school's *expectations* of you when you arrive in terms of what and how much you have to teach. Although the training provider sends the host school information that spell out these requirements, some teachers either fail to read it or do not absorb the detail when they do so. Consequently, it is possible to go to the school on your preliminary visit (also known as the 'initial' or 'pre-visit') in the hope and expectation that you will discover precisely what you need to know, only to be disappointed that things are far less clear-cut.

If your placement starts (say) immediately after the Christmas break with your preliminary visit at the start of the previous December, it is likely that teachers' minds will be more focused on preparations for the coming school play or pantomime than on curriculum matters. Teachers get very tired towards the end of the Autumn Term and this fact, together with the joys and stresses of Christmas, increase the chances that they may not be operating efficiently. Nevertheless, it is important to get as much information about the school's expectations as possible, so that you don't spend the holiday worrying about what might happen and can spend your time more productively. Even so, a lot of detailed negotiation with the teacher or teachers is necessary during the first few days of your main block of school experience. Although it is not easy to approach the class teacher (whom you scarcely know) and request that you both sit down and discuss your timetable in depth, it is essential to do so. Time slips past surprisingly quickly in school and you can discover that opportunities to teach specific subject areas or be closely involved in particular events have been lost.

The encouraging news is that most teachers and school mentors make every effort to discuss your responsibilities with you at the earliest possible time and are only too willing to offer their full support if you are keen to try out something ambitious or new to you. Aurora's enthusiastic comment following her successful time in school is typical of many:

> My class teacher and the two teaching assistants I worked with were excellent, supportive and helpful, giving me ideas, resources and help with researching the topic. My tutor was very experienced and I felt 100% confidence in her guidance. She was kind, supportive and caring, which made the placement so much more pleasurable.

Even under the happiest of circumstances, there is always room for clarification of your role as the placement unfolds and unpredictable factors impact upon decisions; for example, you may take more time to settle than anticipated, or less time; the children may be in the middle of a unit of work that needs to be completed before it is appropriate to hand over fuller levels of responsibility to you; the school may have a special event that requires concentrated, time-consuming rehearsal. Occasionally, the main teacher is ill or absent for other reasons and you have to negotiate with one or more substitute teachers, which tends to delay or accelerate your rise to stardom. Your reaction to unexpected twists and turns also reveals a lot about your suitability for teaching.

Extend your thinking

Make sure that you maintain as much open communication with the teacher and tutor as you endeavour to do with the children.

Making progress on school placement

After the nervous anticipation prior to the start of the placement and the period of orientation during the first few days, your time in school quickly settles into a rhythm and routine. You get to know the children's names and their characters and begin to teach groups, parts of lessons and (as confidence grows) whole lessons. You have opportunities to use stories and discover how difficult it can be to read to children – especially younger pupils – while showing them the pictures in the book. You gain efficiency in the use of technology and may even surprise yourself by the speed with which you learn to handle the practical side of ICT. At the same time you also begin to recognise the limitations of the same technology, especially for very young pupils, who benefit more from touching, holding and manipulating objects than spending their time staring at a screen. You gradually see that teaching is as much a craft and art as it is a technique or set of procedures. You have some uplifting moments and some anxious ones. Your relationship with the host teachers matures. You feel more comfortable about the content of your teaching file as it slowly fills with information about the class, lesson plans, evaluations and assessment information. Typically, Azza was delighted by what she discovered on entering the school, while acknowledging her tentativeness:

> The whole ethos of the school is really friendly and it's nice. The kids are energetic and I'm having a good time, though still finding my feet. I've been with the teacher for a week now and she gave me some really good feedback today, saying that I started very well, so I feel quite good about it. I'm not really too nervous about being in school because the children are nice. The first week's been good: seven more to go!

Deepak had some specific anxieties associated with acceptance and orientating towards the school's prevailing ethos:

> One of the biggest challenges facing the trainee teacher is to integrate successfully into the running of a well-established school, with equally established routines and rules.

And Abraham was tentative about the 'hallowed' nature of the staff room:

> It was not only the classroom responsibilities that gave rise to my anxieties but also other areas of school life; for example, life in the staff room. I was distinctly worried that I would find the staff room to be a 'closed shop' to me.

Brady had forgotten how tiring it is to be in school and how mentally exhausting the job can be, even during the first few days. He also admitted that he had a lingering anxiety about coping:

> I'm dreadfully tired. It's about 7 p.m. and I've just got home from school and it's hit me how much work I've got to do and how tired I am already. I had a good day at school today and taught two lessons; one went a bit a wrong but it wasn't that critical. I'm just feeling a bit exhausted by it all really; a bit brainwashed. I'm fine when I'm at school but when I'm thinking about all the planning and stuff I just get a bit worried. I do enjoy it when I'm there. I just think about it too much.

Lorraine wanted to establish herself with parents as well as with the children and colleagues, but the task proved more difficult than she imagined owing to the parents' preference for the regular class teacher. Note that her account has a twist in the tail.

The parents had already developed a strong bond with the class teacher and they were not particularly interested in me. I attempted to encourage a positive relationship with them by ensuring that I was accessible, approachable, friendly and professional in my conduct. I tried hard to liaise with them in a variety of formal and informal contexts. However, despite all my efforts, I was frustrated to find that at the end of the placement some parents thanked the teacher for the class assembly we had organised when, in truth, I had taken sole responsibility for preparing it. On the final day a parent expressed surprise that I was leaving, as she thought I was there permanently!

Anna quickly acknowledged that she would improve if she persevered with her weaker areas and exploited the stronger ones. She also recognised the importance of maintaining high morale among the pupils after inadvertently giving them a task to do that exceeded their capability:

> On Tuesday I taught literacy but the poems didn't go as well as I'd hoped, mainly because I'd misjudged the task. Although I realised it was a bit tricky at the time for them, the children tried hard and I put positive comments in their books afterwards. I don't feel it was a disaster. I'm realising that if you have a bit of an iffy lesson or they're not too sure about the task, as long as you remain upbeat with them and make the next lesson positive, it's not the end of the world.

You will see from the above comments that adopting a confident approach is very important, aided by practical steps to reinforce the message that you are making progress, of which there are two types: the first is *practical*, such as looking hard at your time management and use of priorities; ensuring that you get sufficient physical exercise; and planning to teach a small amount of curriculum content thoroughly, rather than attempting to cover too much ground and becoming frustrated. The second type of aid is *psychological*, telling yourself that you can succeed and denying yourself the doubtful luxury of self-pity; allowing a trusted friend to offer reassurance; using positive language about a situation; and finding comfort in religious faith or meditation.

Strengthening practice

Make it a habit to pause every evening before leaving school and list five things you have done well. For example:

1   took the register without much hassle
2   the children listened well to my maths introduction
3   helped with playground duty

> 4   completed my assessment task for a target child
> 5   reduced the amount of calling out during the interactive session.

Key issues on placement

Wherever your placement school is located and regardless of the prevailing circumstances, there are universal factors that apply to every situation, such as covering the curriculum, adults and children working together, adherence to a timetable, and so forth. However, it is easy to convince yourself that all your fellow trainees are in a more advantageous position than you. This perception can be skewed, as every situation offers something special and worthwhile. Nevertheless, certain issues will always be significant; and the way that you respond to them is likely to determine the success of your time in school. Thus:

The resident teacher's teaching approach

Some teachers are brash, loud and assertive. They thrive on being out at the front of the class and use a large number of closed questions to keep children on their toes. Other teachers are quiet and intimate. They have gentle voices and maintain order through the use of body language, reminders to the children of what they are supposed to do and expressions of disappointment when they fail to comply. You will be developing your own style but need to be aware of what the children have been used to receiving from their regular teachers. When a class is 'shared' between two teachers it is surprising how widely the teaching approaches differ, yet children seem to be able to accommodate this divergence without undue difficulty after a time. So don't be too anxious if your teaching style is somewhat at variance with the present or previous teacher. The only constant factor should be your attitude towards pupils: transparent, caring, conscientious, insistent about standards of behaviour, flexible in areas where latitude is appropriate and supportively demanding. Here is what Chris experienced when working closely with two teachers:

> The job-share teacher who works at the beginning of the week is really nice and I get on with her. She generally leaves the class when I teach because she's got other things to do and if she does watch me I don't mind because then the children are mine and I can get on with my teaching and get a bit more experience. I'm still a bit unsettled with the second teacher who job-shares but it's improving. I'm getting more confident to talk about how I want to run the classroom, as well as how they want me to do it.

How and when teachers plan their lessons

Many schools have tightly knitted plans to cover the core curriculum for each year group and (usually) rather looser plans in the other subject areas. *Long-term* plans do not particularly concern trainee teachers as they only provide an overview of curriculum coverage from which the *medium-term* plans (often covering half a term) are initially constructed before the teachers that are responsible for each year group include additional information. Some medium-term plans contain highly specific details about lessons, including ideas for pupil activities, use of resources and so forth; other medium-term plans contain little more than a National Curriculum reference and a brief description of the content. The level of planning for *short-term* plans (normally weekly or fortnightly) will depend upon the amount of information already available in the medium-term plan. Teachers also have to take into account the number of colleagues with whom they jointly plan: some schools are one-form entry, so there is only one teacher per year, whereas in larger schools there may be up to three or four parallel classes. For example, it is common for the teachers from the same year group to meet once every two weeks after school to share ideas, clarify strategies that will apply across the classes – e.g. methods of allocating scarce equipment or extension activities for very capable children – and be alert to events and circumstances that might impinge upon lessons (e.g. an extended assembly or singing practice for a forthcoming event). The more deeply involved you become in the teaching programme and the more integral you become to pupil learning, the greater the need for you to engage fully during these planning sessions. These joint-planning sessions do not absolve you from the detailed preparation for each lesson. Ultimately, you have to sit down and do the hard labour of detailing the lesson format from start to finish, including learning objectives, tasks and activities and resources. The joint planning sessions provide a framework but you have to do the hard work in preparing the sessions or parts of sessions for which you have responsibility.

The nature of pupil tasks and activities

Although there are numerous lesson plans and ideas available in electronic and written form, the best teachers are careful to adapt the basic plan and ensure that it is relevant for the children sitting in front of them and not to an 'unknown' audience. As you watch the regular teacher at work, it is useful to make a note of whether she or he tends to:

1   give children a large number of mechanical tasks that allow them to coast through the work without applying their minds
2   organise activities in such a way that there is little additional challenge for pupils who possess the potential to achieve further
3   use work sheets to 'babysit' unattended children

4   have only a vague idea of what the children are intended to *learn* as well as what they will do.

Or by contrast, if the teacher's task management emphasises the following:

5   giving a combination of straightforward tasks and some that require careful thought and decisions
6   providing a range of tasks that allow less able children to succeed, yet provide opportunities for more capable children to extend their learning
7   using work sheets imaginatively
8   helping children to understand what is required of them without being so specifically directed that their learning is constrained.

If any of 1 to 4 apply then you will need to persevere to ensure that you balance the rather predictable and mundane work to which pupils are subjected with opportunities for children to be creative and use their imaginations; for example, through drawing, painting, quizzes and stories about mythical creatures. Another method of counteracting unimaginative practice is to introduce tasks that require children to think deeply and weigh up options; for example, presenting them with choices over how to spend money or making moral decisions. Distinguish the tasks in such a way that all children can tackle some of them and more capable children can move beyond the basic activity. Where possible, incorporate a problem-solving element into the nest of tasks.

In mathematics especially, it is rather too easy to follow a predictable approach of so-called 'mental oral' activities followed by a whole class introduction, followed by differentiated tasks on the basis of ability, followed by a short plenary. Although there is merit in this approach, you can keep the children (and yourself) on their toes by varying the session structure. For instance, begin with a short story in maths, followed by a challenge of the 'How many ways can Goldilocks find to get out of the wood?' or 'How quickly will the camel need to walk if the man is to reach the oasis before the sun gets too hot?' type. One way and another try to ensure that children are kept alert, involved in their learning, encouraged to talk and given a clear focus for the activity. There *is* a place for regularly and systematically working through a series of sums or questions on a work sheet. Every child needs opportunity to work independently, to enjoy the comfort of silence and relish the feel-good factor when correct answers are ticked and a smiley face is awarded. Just make certain that you don't fall into a mechanical and unvarying approach.

It may be that the teacher is highly innovative and imaginative in approach – see points 5 to 8 above – in which case you will need to decide what you are capable of coping with, as some forms of organisation for learning are highly complex and require a lot of experience before being attempted. For instance, systematic use of work sheets and book-based tasks are far easier to manage and assess than investigative activities. In a situation in which pupils have to undertake and complete tasks where the answers are either correct or incorrect, you can spend all your time and energy in monitoring their progress; at the end of the session it is straightforward to mark the answers and record the results on a record sheet. It is much harder to evaluate a collaborative problem-solving task in which the 'right' answer may not be forthcoming and it is difficult to identify individual contributions to the endeavour.

The availability of ICT and software

It is almost certain that the placement school will have a computer suite and a variety of other technological aids. Some host teachers are adept at using equipment within fairly narrow bounds, as required through national initiatives for mathematics and literacy. Others will employ technology as a major resource, both as a support for teaching and to encourage pupils to explore areas of interest, support creative activities and link with remote web sites. It is perfectly possible that you will be more skilled at using ICT than the teacher, in which case you should not feel awkward or pretend to be less knowledgeable than you really are, as it is highly probable that the teacher will warmly welcome your expertise and want to learn from you. However, be aware that every school and teacher has a perspective on the appropriateness of using technology. For instance, some teachers are adamant that innovative activities should be as natural and 'feely' (kinaesthetic) as possible, while others employ technology regularly and creatively to inspire and shape ideas. There may be specific software programs that the teachers have agreed to adopt throughout the school with which you need to familiarise yourself. In day-to-day classroom work there will be opportunities for individual pupils to use a computer, supported in many cases by an assistant. The monitoring of these occasional uses of technology is far from easy and you need to ensure that the assistant gives you regular feedback about how it is working. Some schools are using a variety of technological devices to contact parents about their children's progress (notably: email, web-based forums and texting); if so, you will need to be take advice from the host teachers about procedures and confidentiality.

Strengthening practice

Always have a contingency plan in mind, in case the technology fails.

Large space facilities

Schools vary in the quality of the 'large space' facilities they have available. Whereas larger schools may possess a separate hall largely allocated for use in physical education, dance and drama, smaller schools with only a single large space normally have to accommodate a range of other activities: assembly/act of worship; school meals; parent events, and so forth. The bigger the school population is, the larger the number of classes and the greater the timetable pressures. The fact that children require regular exercise means that during inclement weather there is a heavy demand for hall use. However, large space activities are often great fun, as one trainee noted:

> Had a very good PE session yesterday which was my first one. I've only observed one PE lesson before and assisted in another. I used a candle as a stimulus and made the children pretend to be candles with the flames and the smoke as a precursor for sorting out a dance session and it worked pretty well. So I'm looking forward to tomorrow.

It is more than likely that the school has a policy of promoting 'in-class' physical activities, both as part of a regular programme and used spontaneously. As with every other learning experience, it is wise to start with a straightforward activity, easily managed, and progress to more sophisticated physical exercises when you are established as the teacher and can keep things orderly.

Strengthening practice

Check that the large space is free from potential hazards in advance of the session and not as you begin the lesson. You can ask a TA to confirm that everything is orderly but you must take the final responsibility.

Forthcoming special events

The school timetable largely consists of regular daily sessions that form a structure for curriculum delivery; frequently, the core subjects of literacy and mathematics take place during the morning when children's and teachers' minds are most receptive. Afternoons tend to be used for all other subjects, though PE lessons have to be timetabled throughout the day to accommodate all the class requirements. In addition to the regular sessions there are a number of special events that disrupt the timetable's 'rhythm', classified under three categories:

1   *School-wide events*, such as a History Week, a visiting drama group that performs in front of all the pupils, an assembly led by an important guest, a charity-raising day or a sports' afternoon.
2   *Class-based events*, such as a whole day spent on problem-solving in mathematics or science, a design and technology morning, a visit by older members of the local community to share their experiences of childhood or an investigation of the school grounds and local environment.

3   *Special tuition and coaching events*, such as gifted and talented children visiting a nearby university for a day of challenging experiences; musically able children receiving support from a peripatetic teacher; preparation for an approaching test.

It pays to ask about the onset of special events so that you can adjust your planning accordingly. Even if the event is planned for after you have completed your time in the school, there may still be an impact on the immediate timetable as when, for instance, children need time to practise for an approaching sports' event.

Challenges on placement

Occasionally, a school placement fails to live up to expectations. In a very small minority of cases the experience is disappointing at best and downright unnerving at worst. If you are unfortunate enough to find yourself in an environment that does not suit your temperament it is likely to occur for one or more of the following reasons.

The school is in a state of flux

Sometimes there is a degree of turmoil in school owing to a change of personnel, an impending inspection or a major event, such as a concert or planning for a whole-school 'away day'. There is little that you can do about the situation other than to remain calm, supportive and willing to be flexible, as sudden changes may occur to the timetable and meetings might be called at short notice. Teachers and assistants will be extra busy and the school-based tutor may not spend as much time with you as normal. When you are a qualified teacher you will face similar challenges, so see it as a useful form of preparation for that time.

Your host teacher is unsympathetic

As described earlier in the chapter, the vast majority of teachers entertain trainee teachers because they like working with them. Occasionally, a teacher is coerced into taking a trainee when she or he would rather not do so but, if this is the case, you have access to the school-based tutor, who is almost certainly aware of the class teacher's disposition. He or she may, however, be bound by invisible bonds of loyalty to a colleague with whom he or she has to work long after you have left the school. Despite the divide that you may feel exists between you and the class teacher, nearly all aloof host teachers can be won over if they see that (a) you respond to their advice, (b) you are willing to work hard and (c) you do not pose a threat to their way of working. Don't underestimate the power of (c). When you get your own class you will understand better how difficult it is to hand over the reins to a stranger who wants to do things differently from you. Where the situation is tense, it is inadvisable to suffer in silence, which can lead to mental distress and, in the worst cases, to ill-health, a loss of vocation and even withdrawal from the school experience. Instead, implement the following strategies:

•   Make every effort to convince yourself that the teacher is your ally and not your enemy.
•   Maintain communication channels with the teacher and do not allow yourself to lapse into a resentful silence.
•   Direct your energies towards the children and delight in them.
•   Keep pace with all the training provider requirements, including paperwork, directed tasks and wider school involvement.
•   Find a friendly adult in the school with whom you can have relaxed conversations and informal discussions about the teacher role, though resist the temptation to use the person as someone on whom to pour out your woes.
•   Establish the habit of regularly contacting a sympathetic and level-headed friend (or family member) outside school with whom you can share your frustrations.

It is rare to encounter such a negative attitude but, if you do so, the approach outlined above will carry you through to the end of the placement without unmanageable stress. You will also learn valuable lessons that will be highly beneficial to you in future placements.

You are unused to the age group

Even within the same age phase there are pupils of varying temperament and ability, so when you deal with different age groups there are additional factors to take into account. If you have moved from teaching children in KS2 to KS1 or reception you must remember that younger children do not possess the extended vocabulary of older ones and are more adult-reliant. They take a long time to carry out the tasks that junior aged children do effortlessly. They also have a shorter attention span and cannot hold large amounts of information in their minds. All children benefit in their learning when facts and concepts are reinforced through repetition, the use of visual resources, being taught memory aids (of the 'Every Good Boy Deserves Food' variety to recall the position of notes E, G, B and D in music), memorable poems and ditties, and so on. Younger pupils require tasks that allow for plenty of first-hand experiences; and pupils young and old need opportunities to explore ideas and investigate practical situations; to be amazed by their discoveries and satisfy their curiosities. Older and more capable pupils benefit from time to make in-depth enquiries about a topic, though the teacher has to be careful that they do not compile information without understanding its significance.

The school day tends to be different according to the age group: the timetable for pupils in reception and KS1 is usually more adaptable than in KS2, where setting for ability and the intermingling of children from several classes for mathematics and (perhaps) literacy has to be coordinated. The youngest children will frequently be supervised when they eat their pieces of fruit or drink milk during the morning. Some reception age teachers still insist that a short rest time during the early part of the afternoon is highly beneficial for children, supplemented, perhaps, by playing background music or reading a story. Be assured that however difficult you find it to be initially, you will soon adjust to the new age group until it will seem perfectly natural to be teaching those children.

Extend your thinking

How might your vocabulary differ in expressing approval, encouragement and praise to a five year old, an eight year old and an eleven year old?

You had a disappointing placement last time

Research by Hayes (2004) suggests that one of the key factors affecting a successful school experience is the success of the previous placement. The chances are that you had a happy and fulfilling time. On the other hand, perhaps you heaved a sigh of relief when you left the last school, thankful to have survived it. If so, bear in mind three truths: (a) We learn more from a period of struggling than from a smooth passage, (b) Every new school experience offers a fresh start, (c) The children you are about to teach and the staff with whom you are going to work know little or nothing of your previous time in school, so don't imagine that they do. Make the most of the fresh start.

The class is ill-disciplined

A badly behaved class is a challenge for all new teachers, however competent they may be (see Chapter 6). The host teacher probably has her hands full in coping and there may be specific children who seem incapable of concentrating and responding to an adult's reasonable demands. However, at least three factors weigh in your favour. First, you are not expected to miraculously transform a 'difficult' class of children. Second, you do not have any negative preconceived ideas about the children. Third, it is your opportunity to make your mark by demonstrating that you can motivate the children and keep the mischievous ones on the straight and narrow path. With the present emphasis on individualised learning and inclusion, more assistance is available for children who exhibit anti-social behaviour and/or require special assistance with learning. Nevertheless, it won't all be plain sailing and your daily interaction with the children outside the formal lesson times may hold the key to ultimate success. Have high expectations with regard to children's behaviour and work quality but also be realistic about the amount of time it takes for an under-achieving child to improve. Be patient but insistent; kindly but firm; take the trouble to show the children what needs to be done and how they can do it; explain why certain behaviour is unacceptable and other behaviour is helpful; tell children that they are amazing; be friendly but not 'a friend'; develop a pro-fessionally compassionate attitude, where you engage positively with the troublesome children (liaising with colleagues as you do so) instead of relying on punishments. Measure progress in small steps; the giant strides can wait until you have established your authority and settled into the placement.

The tutor or teacher has unrealistic expectations of you

Occasionally, a tutor or teacher has expectations that far exceed your ability to achieve them and may even interpret your inability as unwillingness or incom-petence, rather than inexperience. In the unlikely instance that you should suffer in this way, it is essential to be open and courteously honest with the tutor. While remaining calm and pleasant, you may want to say something like: 'I am really keen to progress as a teacher and do not mind taking some risks and being stretched but what I am being asked to do is simply beyond my pre-sent level of competence. I need a little more time working on some basic skills and experiencing teaching situations that will allow me to step up my respon-sibilities in the very near future. I'm not trying to avoid facing the challenge you have set me and I am grateful that you have such confidence in me. I want to improve and I want to be a success but I feel a bit out of my depth and need a little more experience before tackling these extended responsibilities.' If you feel nervous about speaking so assertively, show the person this page of the book.

There is confusion about the meaning of working hard

Most trainee teachers are prepared and eager to work very hard. There seems to be an expectation by staff from the host school that you will be sacrificial in the amount of time and effort you put into your preparation for teaching, marking, maintaining records and completion of academic tasks. Some trainees have long journeys or have to live in temporary accommodation close to the placement school in a strange environment without the availabil-ity of resources and an absence of friends. It is little wonder that fatigue takes its toll. First, realise that the time you spend out of school is unseen; you may labour into the early hours of the morning but it won't lead to accolades from the host teachers or tutor. Second, teachers make judgements based on what they observe you doing and not on what you write in your file. Third, the acid test of competence is in the way that you perform during lessons. If you look or sound lethargic from exhaustion caused through over-work out of school it will probably be viewed as inadequacy. Consequently, pay heed to the following:

1   Do not work past 10 p.m. unless it is unavoidable; order your life in such a way that you get a good night's rest.
2   Realise that you cannot compensate for weak teaching by spending hours on completing paperwork and recording pupil data.
3   Think through the session in detail beforehand about the many practical issues that make the difference between a smoothly run and ragged lesson.

You are giving a poor impression to staff

This issue is difficult to explore because it involves the person of 'you'. It is hard to 'stand outside' and see yourself as others see you but even if you are a popular person with many friends and an active social life or you have been commended in the past for your positive manner, it is worth asking some searching questions about your conduct and attitude. The questionnaire below is designed to assist you with the process.

Self-analysis questionnaire

Score these statements with marks from 1 to 5, where 1 is very weak and 5 is very strong:

1   I look on the positive side of life.
2   I see myself as a person of equal worth to everyone else.
3   I trust the word of those who advise me.
4   I listen carefully and show interest when others speak.
5   I smile and laugh a lot.
6   I respond with genuine enthusiasm to people's good ideas.
7   I am tolerant of other people's frailties.
8   I like far more people than I dislike.
9   I try hard to fit in with my colleagues' norms and beliefs.
10 I make every effort to treat my work seriously but not grimly.
11 I keep life in proportion.
12 I am always willing to persevere and do my best.

If you scored between 48 and 60 in the self-analysis questionnaire, you will be welcomed in any school with open arms. If you scored between 36 and 48 you are doing well and have nothing to worry about. If you scored between 24 and 36 it may be helpful to sit down and take a long hard look at yourself with the help of an honest friend. If you scored below 24, seek help urgently.

Turning situations to your advantage

Although each school placement offers wonderful opportunities to become immersed in a school environment and enjoy doing the thing that you most love and enjoy – teaching children – there are also a variety of specific challenges that you might have to confront and overcome, including:

Dealing with lively children

Liveliness is sometimes due to a child's personality or background; sometimes due to an innate brain-related 'wrong-wiring' and sometimes resulting from circumstances, such as a boring lesson, an exciting time of the year or adjusting to a new set of circumstances. In some ways to teach a class that is recognised as more challenging than the average one is advantageous, for at least four reasons. First, you have a chance to demonstrate your resilience. Second, your minor successes are amplified because of the tricky situation in which you are operating. Third, a strong sense of camaraderie often exists amongst the staff that deals with such pupils. Fourth, you gain a considerable amount of satisfaction from small victories and achievements. You may look longingly at your fellow trainee down the road in Angel Wings Primary but there are challenges with every situation. On the other hand, do not imagine that there are simple solutions to what may be deep-seated problems. It is usually necessary to modify your approach in the following ways: (a) Limit the amount of interactive adult–pupil teaching and use transmission methods more often. (b) Give highly specific tasks that individual pupils can handle. (c) Minimise the extent of collaborative work. With older children it is worth organising the furniture formally in rows to reduce the possibility of casual chatter across tables. With younger pupils you need to take special care with resources, as unsettled children can be extremely possessive and may react fiercely if they feel they have been slighted or deprived.

Maintaining a strong self-image

It is perfectly natural to hope that other people think well of you, especially if that person is the tutor or mentor. On the other hand one of the best ways to combat low self-image is to understand that setbacks and even undisguised failures provide the stepping-stones to success. Though it may sometimes seem that you simply cannot please those who need to be convinced about your worth, the chances are that they think much more highly of you than you imagine. Why not ask them? In the meantime remember that your status as a teacher and as a person in your own right is not solely dependent on another person's viewpoint: not even the assessor. Your evaluators possess insight, the ability to analyse situations and offer constructive feedback but they do so imperfectly and may not always express themselves well or be aware how vulnerable you feel.

The most constructive approach you can adopt is to view every comment as an attempt to be helpful and not as a personal slight on your character.

Handling feedback about your teaching

You are entitled to receive regular feedback about the quality of your teaching and, for the most part, you are likely to get a written set of comments from the tutor/mentor and a chance to discuss an observed lesson on at least one occasion per week. While this weekly detailed response is valuable, it is also extremely useful to receive regular feedback from the class teacher if she or he has the time and inclination to do so. Whereas the formal regular observation will provide you with a detailed analysis of your teaching style, subject knowledge and sensitivity to pupils' needs, a less formal but more frequent conversation with the regular class teacher after sessions will allow you to probe not only your teaching skills but also important dimensions of the teacher role, such as the way that you relate to colleagues and parents, time management, tidiness and wider school involvement. A small percentage of teachers and tutors focus their attention on the weaker elements of teaching and neglect to mention the stronger and improving elements, which are usually dominant. If you feel aggrieved with the tone of a lesson report, it is perfectly in order to ask – calmly and without a trace of irony in your voice – which of the stronger aspects of your teaching can be built on; or say (truthfully) that you need advice in listing a few stronger as well as weaker features of your teaching for your lesson evaluation file. This approach will nearly always elicit a helpful response but if it fails to do so you should state quite plainly that you feel very disheartened by the feedback but will do your level best to address the failings over the coming week; then ask the teacher/tutor for some strategies to achieve your aims.

Extend your thinking

In working through delicate situations, ensure that you give a clear message that you accept the criticisms and want to do better in future.

Strengthening practice

Once you have established an easy relationship with the TA, ask her to provide a perspective on a specific aspect of your teaching.

Your placement will never be ideal, for the simple reason that you are in another teacher's classroom, working with pupils whom you have never met before and trying to orientate to the school's procedures and ways of doing things – while being under constant scrutiny. Despite these constraints, the majority of trainees have an enjoyable (if exhausting) time on school experience and feel sad, if a little relieved, when they have to leave and return to academic study.

Strengthening practice

If you find yourself focusing on trivial things too much, picture a giant scale (balance): the irritations sit on the left-hand tray; the positive aspects of the placement sit on the right-hand tray. Make sure that in your thoughts and conversation the scale tips firmly to the right!

Dilemmas in teaching: case studies

Teaching is full of dilemmas and teachers are constantly called upon to make instant decisions about appropriate responses. The following case studies involving trainee teachers are typical of many such examples that require wisdom and discretion. The first five are dealt with briefly; the sixth example is longer and addresses the realities for trainees in classroom situations where discipline and behaviour are serious issues. They are all based on genuine instances, though names have been altered.

Case study 1

Ben is in a Year 6 class in which Alan, a reluctant learner, becomes deeply interested in a local history project and wants to continue working at it after the end of the timetabled session. Ben is delighted at the child's newly found motivation but anxious that the more he allows him to choose what he does, the more difficult it will become to insist that he engages with less appealing areas of learning. Furthermore, a few of the other reluctant learners are starting to protest that Alan is given preferential treatment.

ADVICE TO BEN

Commend Alan warmly. Offer to find him some time very soon to continue work on the topic. Tell the other children that you are pleased with Alan because he has worked quickly and made a real effort, so is being rewarded fairly. Explain that if they want similar treatment, they must show equal determination. Maintain the dialogue with Alan about his interest (which may wane quite quickly). Reward his endeavours. Tell the class teacher in front of Alan about how sensible he has been. You may be anxious that some of the children who always work hard may be envious; experience suggests that a quiet word with them in a 'grown-up' way about what you are doing to help Alan will take care of that concern.

Case study 2

Linda was concerned because the class teacher, Mrs Hogshorn, with whom she was placed, did little planning and spent a lot of time 'on her feet' talking to an increasingly restless group of six year olds, who seemed unwilling to risk being overtly naughty. Linda's main point of concern was that her own teaching style relied on involving children in their learning by encouraging them to contribute ideas, offer suggestions and explore solutions. She was afraid that the contrast between her own and the teacher's approach would unsettle the children and might cause friction.

ADVICE TO LINDA

Make haste slowly. Gradually implement your own approach but make constant reference to what Mrs Hogshorn has told the children and taught them as you do so. Don't be apologetic about your approach. Try a little didactic (direct) teaching to hone your skills in this direction. Don't become a 'one-method' teacher: instead, make sure you have a range of teaching strategies in your armoury. Keep discussing your teaching strategies with Mrs Hogshorn.

Case study 3

Desmond was placed in a Year 4 class with a relatively new teacher and an older TA, who had worked at the school for many years. The TA often called across the room, admonishing individuals and barking out commands. The teacher, Mr Wellock, seemed in awe of the assistant and did not seek to counteract her brisk manner. Desmond wondered how he was going to cope with the assertive TA when even the class teacher allowed her to dominate.

ADVICE TO DESMOND

Befriend the TA, even if she initially seems unresponsive. Be open with the regular teacher by asking advice about how best to use the TA's skills most effectively. Do not, of course, give the slightest hint what you secretly think about Mr Wellock's meek attitude. Continue to plan your lessons normally, including a role for the TA. Include her from time to time in your comments when you are addressing the children and thank her warmly for her contribution. Ask her if she would like to be involved in other ways. In the unlikely event that the situation becomes unmanageable, seek advice discretely from the school mentor but on no account make an enemy of a TA.

Case study 4

Ellen was puzzled about how to handle a small group of mischievous Year 5 boys, who appeared to find everything amusing. Even the slightest deviation from the norm triggered immature behaviour: giggles, glances at one another and silly facial expressions. The class teacher kept admonishing them and sent them to see the deputy head on a number of occasions but although it made some difference in the short term, the silliness gradually returned. In fact, nothing that the teacher did seemed to make a lasting difference. When the teacher eventually refused to allow them to participate in games as a punishment for their poor attitude, they became resentful and started to 'work to rule' by taking more time over the tasks than they needed and feigning confusion about how to complete the activities.

ADVICE TO ELLEN

Confront the behaviour directly. Make sure that seating arrangements make it difficult for the boys to have a clear view of one another. Avoid making a spectacle of them, such that they receive attention from other class members. Take opportunities to work more closely with one boy at a time away from his pals with an interesting activity to subtly coax him away from the influence of his co-conspirators. If possible, arrange with one of the KS1 teachers for one of the boys to go to her class to assist with reading; do not say anything to him about the action being a reward or a punishment. If asked by another child about why it is happening, be honest about the reason; if one of the other 'naughty' boys asks if he can do the same thing, say that you'll see what you can do. (Rather paradoxically, silly boys often respond well to opportunities to do something constructive and behave more sensibly as a result of being given responsibility.) Find out what the boys really enjoy and begin to create in their minds that you are a possible source of preferment towards them spending time on that area – but don't be seen as a softy. Such children won't ever behave perfectly but the situation should improve to the point where you can be relaxed together with them without compromising your authority.

Case study 5

Kath was a bit overwhelmed when she went to work in the Year 2 class to which she was allocated. Her previous school experience had been in a rural school with only five teachers, two part-time TAs and a school administrator. This time the school was in a densely packed conurbation; class sizes were high and there were a large number of additional staff involved in 'boosting standards' by removing pupils from the class for special help and support. Kath found it difficult to get to know the children's names and even harder to begin to create the sense of community that she longed to see, as individuals were regularly being removed from the room by the support staff: one child for additional reading; another child to practise some maths that he had missed; yet another to be coached in … Kath did not know quite what. Pupils taken out of the room took time to become re-absorbed into the lesson when they returned and she found it necessary to deviate from her teaching for a few moments to explain to each child what was happening. It seemed to Kath like organised chaos.

ADVICE TO KATH

It takes time to orientate to a new situation. Some classroom routines flow silk-ily from start to finish; others bump along and scramble over the finishing line. Don't be dismayed by the apparently topsy-turvy conditions. Some teachers and children thrive in a loosely organised structure, *providing* they know their own place and role. Trouble begins for all concerned when pupils are uncertain about expectations and feel at the mercy of circumstances; but don't confuse orderliness with efficiency or disorderliness with ineptness. If you are the 'neat and tidy' kind of person, you will gradually be able to systematise the proceed-ings and improve the overall quality of organisation. Such changes will happen gradually; in the meantime go about your work with a smile on your face and enjoy the ride. You will probably find that after a few weeks the apparent chaos makes perfect sense and you wouldn't have classroom life any other way.

Case study 6

Finally, here is a double case study about two trainee teachers, Sinead and Yana, facing similar, but contrasting challenges in their placement schools. These two examples of how the trainees coped with their situations show that it is impor-tant to persevere and grapple with issues until a successful outcome is reached, rather than take a fatalistic view that nothing can change. First, Sinead discov-ers with her Year 4 class that adopting the regular teacher's use of rewards and sanctions sits uneasily with her desire to develop a more relational climate:

> As soon as I arrived in the school, the class teacher provided me with guid-ance about how I could assert myself. Her advice focused on the use of discipline and issues to do with class control, which she perceived to be essential abilities for anyone aspiring to be 'the teacher'. At first I relied on these strategies to encourage the children to accept me as the person in charge. I made explicit my expectations about their behaviour and began to be insistent about them responding in the way I expected. However, I became uneasy that my positive relationship with the children might be hindered if I continued with this stern approach. I worried that the chil-dren might become intimidated and fail to learn effectively as a result and that in my attempts to dominate the class I was erecting a barrier between me and them. As a result, I began to place more emphasis on being

friendly and listening to what they had to say, without compromising my position of authority. The positive response from the children encouraged me to believe that they were gradually accepting me as their teacher. This fact increased my confidence about my ability to be a good teacher.

It is important to emphasise that although Sinead decided to adopt a different approach, she made sure that the class teacher was fully aware of her intentions and made allowance for some initial turbulence as the children adjusted to the change. If Sinead had proceeded without being open, the teacher might have concluded that she was behaving recklessly by ignoring advice.

The second and more comprehensive account that follows about Yana's experience in a Year 1 class is instructive in four ways. First, it shows that even more experienced teachers don't necessarily have all the answers. Second, that a partnership between trainee and host teacher can be very productive. Third, that there is no 'magic' solution to handling challenging classes. Finally, that thoughtful perseverance brings its own reward.

During the first few days in school it was evident that the class of Year 1 children was quite a handful. Registration was interrupted by a lot of chatter and restless behaviour. I was not sure whether the teacher hadn't noticed what was going on or chose to ignore it, so I did not intervene. However, the poor behaviour continued throughout the day and the teacher kept raising her voice to be audible. Children shouted across the tables to each other when they were doing group activities and the noise level was very high. I was asked to work with the shared reading group during literacy sessions but found that the volume of noise made it impossible to hear properly.

The class had obviously been having the run of things for a considerable length of time and it was now the Spring Term. How on earth was I going to manage if a more experienced teacher had problems? The class teacher was a bit embarrassed and apologetic, explaining that they had been the same in reception and had never settled down. I went home feeling depressed and anxious about how I was going to handle the situation. I decided to consult with my school-based mentor and the tutor from the faculty. Unfortunately, they offered conflicting advice: the mentor told me to be very firm and establish control as quickly as possible before I would be in a position to make progress in my teaching; the tutor cautioned that I should be wary of adopting a different approach from the teacher for fear of confusing the children. What was I to do? I decided that the mentor was more familiar with the situation and so took her advice.

The next time I met the class was when I read them a story and I used the occasion as an opportunity to lay down the rules and my expectations of them. I explained how I wanted them to concentrate on what I was saying and to sit still. I warned them about my quiet voice and the need for them to listen carefully. I told them about my very good eyes that could see everything that was going on in the room. After making sure that they understood what I was saying I continued with the story and was aware that a number of the children were watching me intently to see if I meant what I said and I finished the story without interruption. Even the children seemed surprised at how well they had behaved though, to my disappointment, the class teacher made no comment.

Over the following days I tactfully suggested to the class teacher my ideas for improving class behaviour and with her approval and support initiated some changes. We identified three key areas that were causing significant disruption: (1) noise levels, (2) the transition between activities and (3) the children's inability to stop and listen on request. Over the next few weeks, and not without frustration, effort, tears, joy, anger, exhaustion, lots of discussion and, most of all, patience, the children and I began to understand one another better. By week 4, we reached a level of communication by which a little glance and the 'wait a moment' look was usually – though by no means always – sufficient to nip the action in the bud. It was only after this point had been reached that I was able to focus more on learning objectives, assessment of children's progress and related issues. Class control and management remained a challenge but much less so than beforehand.

The benefits of spending time establishing control and cementing a positive relationship with the children only became fully evident during the last couple of weeks in school. I was so thrilled when one little girl, who had previously been shy and reluctant to come to school, came up to me as she was leaving to go home and said that she had enjoyed the day and liked coming to school now.

Notice that whereas Sinead decided to adopt a more relaxed approach that contrasted with the somewhat repressive system used by the regular teacher, Yana used a stern strategy that contrasted with the regular teacher's lax style. However, both decisions were shown to be correct. Note the following key points:

- The situations looked initially unpromising but were, in fact, capable of resolution.
- The trainees took advice and intelligently weighed up the options.
- Decisions took account of a moral dimension as well as hard practicalities: to tolerate the existing situation would create fewer problems for the trainees in negotiating with the teacher but increase their inner turmoil.
- The situations improved gradually but included setbacks and were never perfect.
- The trainees ultimately felt more relaxed and satisfied as a result of taking decisive action.

There isn't a practitioner in the world, regardless of how experienced and highly rated, who has a solution to every problem and responds to every situation ideally. Every teacher – new or old – has to be willing to learn, persevere and hone the many skills attached to the job. In addition, rather like an athlete, it is necessary to constantly practise techniques, research new ideas, evaluate strategies and set fresh but realistic targets for self-achievement.

Equally important, however, is to imitate for your *own* learning the same positive attitude that you adopt with children when you help them with the things they find difficult but also encourage them to build on the things they already do well. Treat your personal development similarly; see the professional learning exercises in Chapter 10.

Professional learning perspectives

First meeting with a new class

Medwell (2007, pp. 29–30) stresses the importance of a trainee teacher's behaviour when meeting the class for the first time. Thus:

> Whatever class you are placed in, your first step will be meeting the class teacher and simply watching the class for a day, perhaps helping children to complete tasks. Your introduction to the class is very important. The children will use your title (Mr, Mrs, Miss) and surname (unless first names are used for all teachers in school) and the teacher will tell the children you will be teaching them for some of this term. You must look confident and relaxed, however terrified you feel, and fill the role of teacher as you are introduced.

Medwell goes on to offer advice about the importance of body language:

> Stand up straight and keep your arms relaxed (it may help to hold a file or something to stop you nervously clasping your hands). Smile – a relaxed, authoritative smile is appropriate, not a nervous whimper or a rictus grin (a fixed open-mouthed expression of horror). Any time you say something it must be confident and authoritative… First impressions count and you need to signal to the class that you know what you are doing – even if you are not really that sure of yourself.

Teacher role behaviour

The description below (slightly modified) is based on information from a book written many years ago by Eric Hoyle (1969, pp. 59–60) who claimed that the classroom behaviour of teachers is characterised by a variety of roles, as follows:

1 *Representative of society*: inculcating moral precepts.
2 *Judge*: assessing work and giving marks, grades and feedback.

3   *Resource*: possessing knowledge and skills required by pupils.
4   *Helper*: providing guidance when pupils are in difficulty.
5   *Referee*: settling disputes.
6   *Detective*: discovering rule-breakers.
7   *Object of identification*: possesses traits for children to imitate.
8   *Limiter of anxiety*: helps children to control their impulses.
9   *Ego-supporter*: helps children to have confidence in themselves.
10   *Group leader*: establishes and maintains the classroom climate.
11   *Parent surrogate*: seen as a substitute mum or dad.
12   *Target for hostilities*: acts as an object of aggression.
13   *Friend and confidante*: establishing warm relationships with children.
14   *Object of affection*: meets the psychological needs of children.

Find out more by reading

Hayes, D. (2003) *A Student Teacher's Guide to Primary School Placement*, London: Routledge.
Overall, L. and Sangster, M. (2007) *Primary Teacher's Handbook*, London: Continuum.

Chapter 9

Prospering as a trainee teacher

The content of Chapter 9 includes:

- lesson preparation advice, working with other adults and coping with paperwork
- strategies for establishing and cementing your authority
- characteristics that are needed to be a very competent teacher
- extra-curricular involvement
- examples of trainees excelling on school placement.

Points to consider as you read this chapter:

1 The range of attributes and qualities required by effective trainee teachers.
2 Ways to ensure that you remain abreast of the essential demands and requirements made of trainee teachers.
3 How to become an excellent practitioner.

Lesson planning and preparation

Regardless of how well meaning you are and how much you enjoy working with children, there is no substitute for thorough lesson planning and preparation. The two terms 'lesson planning' and 'preparation' have subtly different meanings. Lesson planning is, as its name implies, the process of producing an action plan for a teaching session in the pursuit of pupil learning. Preparation involves lesson planning *plus* harnessing resources *plus* rehearsing the predicted progress of the lesson in your head *plus* mental adjustment to secure a sound emotional state of mind prior to the start of the session.

A lesson is a structured means for helping children to organise their thinking, acquire knowledge, practise skills and understand the world better. All lesson planning must therefore take account of three factors:

1   what the children already know and understand
2   what the children need to know and understand
3   the best way to help them move from point 1 to point 2.

The way that lessons are structured and organised will vary according to the subject area and purpose; for instance, a formal lesson might involve you doing nearly all of the talking and the pupils doing most of the listening, followed by a period in which the pupils work individually at tasks. At the other end of the scale, the lesson might be a 'big space' games session on the school field, where factors such as health and safety and correct use of equipment are important considerations. Regardless of the circumstances, there are some basic principles that apply to every circumstance:

- Use a systematic approach, assisted by an outline lesson pro forma (normally supplied by college or school).
- Concentrate on the things that you want the children to learn or experience.
- Incorporate tasks and activities that will help to fulfil the lesson intentions.
- Specify the links with the formal curriculum or other relevant documentation.
- Identify key vocabulary and questions, allowing time for children to submit queries.
- State how you intend to assess the children's progress.
- Specify the resources that will be needed.
- Write down the anticipated lesson process, step by step, including the introduction, the main body of the lesson and the conclusion (see Chapter 7).
- Ensure that your plans take account of the learning needs of different children or groups, including the more able pupils and children with limited spoken or written English.

Extend your thinking

The curriculum should not only be covered but also uncovered and discovered.

The role of other adults in lessons

An increasingly significant part of your role is to liaise with the TAs who support children's learning and help to shape their emotional and social development (Cheminais, 2008). In earlier chapters we noted that a TA can be a source of moral and practical support, inspiration and wisdom for adults as well as pupils. It isn't always easy to find time to liaise with the TA and let her or him know your plans and expectations, but you must find a means to do so.

The presence of support staff allows you to work more imaginatively, for the following reasons:

- The availability of the assistant allows you to be more flexible in the way that you organise for learning.
- Having assistants gives you opportunities to be the team leader.
- A capable assistant can release you to concentrate on the higher order skills associated with the job.
- An assistant who is knowledgeable in a particular curriculum area can provide expertise that complements your own.

She or he may possess specific expertise in a subject area such as ICT (see Galloway, 2007) or spend valuable time with a child who is struggling with an aspect of school life, such as behaviour, concentration on tasks or relating to others in the class or playground. Some salaried assistants have quite a lot of teaching experience (especially Higher Level Teaching Assistants, HLTA), who may be considered more akin to an assistant teacher than to a TA. Other assistants are parent helpers (the majority of whom are female) with varying degrees of experience and know-how. Your responsibility is fourfold:

1   to develop a harmonious relationship with the assistant by being courteous, initiating conversations and being interested in her welfare
2   to find out from the class teacher about any agreed tasks that the assistant regularly handles and expects to continue doing so
3   to let the assistant know in broad terms what you are hoping to do with the children during a given session
4   to ensure that the assistant is clear about the role you would like her to play during that session.

Assistants do not need or wish to know all the lesson details – that is your business – but will appreciate being involved and informed about procedures in such a way that it helps them feel relaxed and gives them a fair chance to use their expertise.

Extend your thinking

Anything significant that you say to a parent helper might be repeated outside the school. Be wise about the way that a teasing remark or dry humour or generalisation about pupil ability or comment about the school set-up may be interpreted if shared with others.

Strengthening practice

Ask an assistant to observe closely one 'key' child during an interactive phase between you and the pupils and note broadly the length of time that: (a) the child is obviously paying close attention, (b) the child is obviously not paying attention, (c) the child is unsettled. Record and use this information to aid future classroom practice.

Managing paperwork

Almost every practitioner complains about paperwork. It is certainly true that owing to the emphasis on 'evidence-based' practice there has been a significant increase in recordkeeping and maintaining a 'paper trail'. The availability of a designated time for preparation, planning and assessment for teachers (often referred to as 'PPA time') has resulted in a heightening of expectation about the level of detail about lessons and learning outcomes that are committed to paper. Schools are becoming increasingly transparent with regard to all aspects of their role, including the requirement to keep parents closely informed about the progress of their children; consequently, teachers feel obliged to keep detailed records that will facilitate the communication process.

As a trainee teacher you will also be expected to complete a reflective journal of your own progress as a teacher and the things you have learned by teaching or observing others teach. Some trainees prefer to use a narrative form; others list key statements under bullet points; yet others prefer diagrammatic representations – or a combination of methods. The act of writing something down necessitates decisions about priorities and drawing from evidence, rather than making random 'wishful thinking' comments; as such, the maintenance of an orderly, well-informed and accessible school experience file benefits your professional development and allows you to demonstrate that you are fulfilling the school experience requirements.

Strengthening practice

To keep paperwork under control, categorise your teaching file under four broad headings:

1   What you are doing as a teacher during lessons.
2   What you are achieving as a teacher during lessons.
3   What pupils are doing during lessons.
4   What pupils are achieving during lessons.

Exerting your authority

The greatest challenge for every inexperienced teacher is establishing and maintaining discipline. If children are misbehaving, then all your best-laid plans, visual effects, dynamic personality and exciting lessons are frittered away in an atmosphere of tension and struggle. Thorough planning, appropriate use of ICT and other aids, a lively approach and interesting content reduce the likelihood that disruption will occur. Although these features will not, of themselves, guarantee a calm and purposeful atmosphere, their *absence* will invite poor behaviour.

Some trainee teachers imagine that getting angry is a suitable vehicle for expressing firmness about what is appropriate. They may also try to speak formally and artificially to give the impression that they are in charge. In fact, authority is not an automatic right of every adult and has to be earned rather than imposed. While the large majority of children give a new teacher a few days of grace before they start to test the boundaries of what is allowable, you cannot permit too much time to pass before exerting your authority. Quite simply, if you are too chummy in the early days of meeting a class, you run the risk of being viewed as a 'big child' and, when you need to be firm, the children will find it difficult to adjust to your new role as an authority figure. If you are too heavy-handed initially you will almost certainly invite resentment and, even if the children are too scared to be openly naughty, they will find ways to pay you back.

Strengthening practice

Speak with the same courtesy to the children as you do to your colleagues.

Teacher action and pupil reaction

- If you are too fierce in the first encounters you invite fear and resentment.
- If you are too tentative you invite derision.
- If you vacillate between fierceness and tentativeness you will create uncertainty and confusion.

The more that you give the firm impression that you are not only directing and instructing, but also that you have the *right* to do so, the quicker the children will accept you as leader and obey naturally. A lot depends on the way that the regular teacher behaves: if she steps in and 'rescues' you every time the situation becomes tricky, you will have difficulty in being taken seriously by the children. If you can agree with her that she remains in the background and only intervenes when you request it, such a policy offers you the space and opportunity to get to grips with challenging situations. The most useful strategy that the teacher can employ when children turn to her for guidance and arbitration is to remind them that *you* are presently in control, so they must ask you first. Although this level of responsibility can be quite daunting initially, it is ultimately the only way to secure your position as classroom leader.

While your aim is to develop a situation in which children comply sensibly out of respect for you as the senior figure, you don't want to crush the vitality out of children. As with so many aspects of the teacher's role, you should strive to maintain a balance between spontaneity and getting the set work finished; between drawing from the natural enthusiasm and energy of individuals and ensuring that each child has a fair chance to contribute and learn.

Look and sound like a teacher

Teachers' appearance has little to do with their clothing, though children seem to respond well to brighter colours. The 'look' of a teacher has more to do with the person's bearing (how they walk and stand) and their body language: good eye contact, responsive gestures and open body position. To sound like a teacher necessitates crystal clear speech and not 'swallowing' words or sounding breathless due to poor breathing (usually as a result of anxiety). Real teachers convey a strong impression to children that they know what they are talking about and will not be fazed by circumstances. As Killick (2007) rightly comments:

> We communicate our attitudes and our relationships through our posture, facial expression, eye contact, tone of voice and physical proximity. We communicate our feelings through our actions far more than through our words and we can learn more about what someone is feeling by looking at what their body is saying. (p. 93)

In particular, if you have a sharp sense of humour it is important to realise that not everyone has the capacity to distinguish between dry humour and sarcasm, and between witty remarks and superciliousness. Be happy and lively but allow the existing staff to set the tone; they are in charge.

Strengthening practice

Regular breathing practice will help you to speak more naturally and smoothly. Standing upright, with feet apart, breathe in gently through the nose for a count of four and allow air to travel deep into your lungs. Keep your shoulders relaxed as you do so. Hold the breath for a slow count of four and then slowly release it through your mouth for a count of four. Repeat the process, counting to six, then eight, then ten as you release the air. You will be amazed at the effectiveness of this one-minute exercise if carried out several times each day.

Anticipate problems

You will note that this sub-heading invites you to anticipate and not to *expect* problems. If you base your teaching career on fear about what might happen, you will be miserable; if you think through the session carefully in advance and organise things in such a way that the likelihood of disruption is minimised, you will grow increasingly confident as the session unfolds. It is particularly important to make a solid start to the lesson by insisting that children are paying attention (be brisk but friendly; use a small bell or countdown from 5 to 1); ensure that they are listening (see under 'Varying your tone and speed of delivery', p. 126) and announce the purpose of the session, with broad-brush detail about what the children will be expected to do later on. As noted above, make sure that the TA not only knows what is happening but also her role in the proceedings; otherwise she or he may be redundant during the opening lesson phase.

One potential disruption point is at lesson junctures. For example, if you are sending children from the carpet to tables (especially if it is via trays to pick up pencils and books), send a few at a time but keep the flow of children moving. Avoid turning your back on pupils when actively teaching but be careful that writing on the board 'at an angle' does not become a scrawl. Where possible, have words and phrases and simple facts written up on cards or electronically before the lesson. Make sure that the resources are accessible, fairly distributed and in good order. If children are working on a practical activity, see that they have adequate space, or boundary disputes can quickly emerge. Don't allow a gaggle of mischievous children to work together. One way and another take preventative rather than remedial action.

Strengthening practice

In addition to your regular teaching, use opportunities such as taking the register, dismissing the class, leading them to and from the hall and meeting parents at the door to emphasise your authority and status.

Take account of attention spans

On the assumption that you will have children in your class with attention spans that range from 'very limited' to 'extensive' (see Chapter 6), it is a challenge to provide a learning climate in which the weaker ones strengthen their concentration and participation and the stronger ones are not hindered from further development. To find out pupils' attention spans, begin by reading or telling a short story about a dilemma or challenge or decision faced by an imaginary child. Invite comments from the children and ask gentle but searching questions, while keeping your tone as normal and conversational as possible to avoid giving the impression that you are 'testing' them. Ask the TA to take close note of different children's contributions (see earlier) and after several such sessions, allocate the children to one of the following categories:

- paid little attention, fidgeted, distracted other children
- listened but did not contribute in any way
- only repeated comments made by other children
- made occasional single utterance original contributions
- made extended original contributions
- added to a contribution made by another child
- argued for and against comments made by others
- applied principles from the discussion to related situations.

On the basis of these observations you can begin to modify your active teaching to take account of the children's disposition; for example, you can make some allowance for restless children and gently encourage shy ones. It is also useful to see whether the attention span of individuals during teacher-class interactive sessions is the same for them during formal task work: some children prefer to 'get their heads down' than participate during interactive phases; others behave in quite the opposite way.

Strengthening practice

When deciding how to engage children's interest, ask yourself what kinds of things excite a child of that age. They are likely to include events such as parties, outings to the seaside or fair, visiting a grandparent or a friend's house for tea, playing in a sports' team, pursuing a hobby or going on holiday. See how many ways you can exploit such interests in your lessons.

Achieving high levels of competence

If all you had to do as a teacher in training was to 'meet' the Q-standards by providing specific evidence that you had neatly acquired each of them, every teacher would be equally competent and effective. However, it is clearly the case that the degree of competence varies considerably from one qualified person to another, so there must be something more to competence than mere compliance.

There are many factors involved in determining teaching effectiveness: not only having adequate subject knowledge but also an understanding of how children learn and ways to raise pupil motivation and foster enthusiasm. Equally, your willingness to 'get stuck in', respond enthusiastically to the opportunities given to you and play your part as a team member make a considerable difference to the way in which you are treated by colleagues and your own self-confidence. In achieving these goals, every trainee teacher who wants to prosper as a teacher should endeavour to cultivate and enhance the following:

- Be active around the room.
- Be discriminating in offering help.
- Pay attention to detail.
- Gradually assume teaching responsibilities.
- Talk with and not at the children.
- Care but don't pamper.
- Show the right sort of determination.
- Satisfy the host teacher.
- Analyse and reflect on practice.
- Accept advice thoughtfully.

Be active around the room

It is important to show your colleagues and tutors that you are enthusiastic about the job, but excessive fervour can be counter-productive if it creates a feverish atmosphere that transmits to the children and creates difficulties for over-excitable youngsters. Manic behaviour is characterised by very rapid speech, superficial engagement with content and flitting from one thing to another in an attempt to maintain (supposedly) a good pace. There *are* occasions when a powerful tempo engages the children, raises expectation and creates a feeling that learning is fun; for example, a short burst of questions based on number computations or spellings or a set body of knowledge can rescue a session from mediocrity. On the other hand, when issues need to be explored, concepts reinforced and ideas shaped, a depth of understanding emerges from a combination of careful explanation (often supported visually), questions that cause pupils to think about the range of alternatives or options, and tasks to reinforce the learning or to extend it through problem solving/investigation. Your enthusiastic handling of the curriculum content needs to create the right motivating conditions without leaving you, and them, feeling exhausted.

Strengthening practice

Record a section of your lesson and pay particular attention to the quality of your diction and the resonance ('ringing quality') of your voice. See if there are places you should have paused for breath.

Be discriminating in offering help

Most children ask for assistance from an adult at some point during the lesson, though a small number prefer to struggle on unaided. You will, of course, be keen to offer help and guidance, but also to use the opportunity to extend children's thinking by asking supplementary questions, probing their understanding and offering alternatives. If you offer too much help, too readily, there is a risk of children using you as a substitute for doing their own thinking. If you are too tentative, children may get demoralised or fear to ask you for assistance, lest you ply them with hard questions or imply that they should be able to work it out for themselves. Younger pupils, in particular, easily become distressed if they believe that the teacher is being unhelpful. There is a fine balance to be achieved between 'telling' and 'prompting'. In general, a procedural question (do we have to do this or that?') should be answered directly and plainly; a question about alternatives ('shall I do this way or that way?') invites you to help children make up their own minds; a speculative question ('how shall I sort out this problem?') is best met by asking the child a series of questions to expose the issues in advance of finding a solution.

Strengthening practice

When you suspect that a child may know or be capable of finding out without your assistance, use the following strategy: first, show interest in what the child is doing; second, affirm what the child has already accomplished; third, offer a prompt and, if that does not work, suggest that the child ask a friend or direct the child to the source of information; fourth, if the child is still struggling, provide the answer and add an encouraging comment before moving your attention elsewhere.

Pay attention to detail

If you are still inexperienced as a teacher, it is essential to imagine the lesson beforehand and 'rehearse' it in your mind. Ideally, the mental rehearsal should be carried out in the classroom or hall where the lesson will take place so that you can envisage the location of resources, seating positions of children and physical factors such as visibility and access to the board or equipment. You could compare such preparation with the way that a film (a 'movie') is produced by first creating a storyboard, in which the main elements of the film are sketched out and placed in running order so that the producer and team can chart the overall sequence (see Table 9.1). Initially, trainee teachers rely heavily on the lesson plan to carry them safely through the allocated time, but after a while it can be set aside and they rely on a summary of key points written on a notepad or even hand written on a large sheet of paper attached to the wall

Table 9.1 Lesson storyboard

1	2	3	4	5
Links made with previous learning and introduction to present lesson	Interactive session using questions and answers	Use of different media to illustrate points	Explaining tasks and activities	Supervising tasks and activities
6	7	8	9	10
Intervening to provide fuller explanations and clarify misconceptions	Giving a warning about task completion	Reviewing the lesson, celebrating and summarising key learning	Tidying work and ensuring that resources have been returned	Dismissing the class in an orderly fashion

opposite. Eventually, you will do without detailed notes altogether because the 'blueprint' of the session will be securely locked in your head. Once the session begins it is difficult to look at your lesson plan, so view it as a vehicle rather than a crutch.

Strengthening practice

Using the section 'Teacher action and pupil reaction' on p. 172   as a guide, add details as appropriate for the lesson.

Gradually assume teaching responsibilities

If you have already taken responsibility for the whole class you will know just how overwhelming it can be to feel 30 pairs of eyes boring into your face. Many trainees speak of a wave of emotion close to panic sweeping through them, tempting them to break free from its grip by speeding up the lesson, speaking quickly or ending the interactive phase prematurely and moving on to the more easily managed task phase. Other trainees thrive on public exposure and relish the influence they exert, especially when on their feet at the front of the room. Whatever your disposition, keep firmly in mind the principle that even if you are a confident person and raring to 'get stuck in', it pays to be wary about accepting teaching responsibility for which you are poorly prepared. On the other hand it is essential that the host teacher or tutor does not get the impression that you are shying away from the more demanding teacher roles out of timidity. Being cautious but not hesitant requires a cool evaluation of your progress and experiences thus far and ways to gain wider exposure to situations without experiencing undue mental anguish.

> ### Strengthening practice
>
> If you are new to the school or to the subject area, negotiate with the teacher to take responsibility for a *portion* of the lesson/session instead of assuming complete command immediately. For instance, you might lead the 'warm up' phase in PE or take charge of the lesson review (so-called 'plenary') for the final 10 or 15 minutes of a maths lesson.

Talk with and not at children

If you talk *at* children you will see a wall of attentive but blank faces. Helping each child to feel that you are 'sitting alongside' him or her when you speak and make eye contact will extend attention span and is more likely to engage interest. Watch a skilled teacher or assistant at work and you will observe the expressiveness and use of 'you' and 'we' in much of what is said. Adult–pupil interaction is strengthened by the use of occasional rhetorical questions ('thinking aloud'), by flashes of humour and variation in the speed and pitch of delivery. You cannot, of course, learn *for* the children, so you must motivate them to want to do so by speaking to them in a way that not only informs but also has them thirsting to know more.

> ### Strengthening practice
>
> A Chinese proverb claims: 'Tell me and I forget. Show me and I remember. Involve me and I understand.' But an alternative version might be: 'Tell me *with enthusiasm* and relate it to my experience and I am unlikely to forget. Show me *using a variety of interesting visual aids* and I remember and want to share with others. Involve me and provide support, encouragement and the appropriate skills that I need, and I *release my creativity*. Do all three things and help me to understand my place in the world and the place of others, and I am truly educated.' See Chapter 1.

Care but don't pamper

Some people argue that it is possible to care too much and in so doing to invite distress and damage to the trainee's well-being. The reason for such caution is that as your influence has a limited effect on pupils' lives, you cannot hope to transform every child's situation. By contrast, others claim that the principle of caring is the essence of teaching because its absence would lead to a mechanical approach that is more conducive to working with machines or computers than with flesh and blood children. As is commonly the case, the truth lies somewhere between these two extremes. It is essential to care, but to care about the *right things* and in the *right way*, such that you are better able to help children:

- receive an effective and relevant education that will allow them to pass formal tests and cope with the everyday demands of life
- mature into responsible and compassionate citizens, with a positive, selfless view of life
- respond positively to challenging circumstances and possess the confidence to find solutions.

This threefold caring (knowledge, responsibility and self-reliance) must not be confused with 'pampering', where you become over-protective and do not allow your pupils a chance to experience challenge, difficulty and failure. In such a case, your desire to help mould learners tends instead to create 'mouldy' learners – weak-willed and lacking tenacity – deprived of the chance to build character and enjoy the exhilaration of success achieved through perseverance. It is not always easy to walk the line between caring and pampering, but if you make pupil self-dependency your ultimate aim, you won't go far wrong.

Strengthening practice

Make children feel by your positive reaction that what is important to them is important to you.

Show the right sort of determination

There are two forms of determination, one of which is worth possessing, the other which is not. The sort of determination that you should *avoid* having is the relentless variety, where you doggedly stick at doing something in a particular way because you started it and do not intend to stop. The blinkered approach is certainly steadfast but ultimately self-defeating for the simple reason that it takes no account of changing circumstances and prevents an intelligent evaluation of the strategies that you are employing. The second form of determination is a worthwhile one, where you do not allow temporary setbacks to deter you from improving your teaching and professional commitments, but learn from your mistakes, ask advice and persevere to improve your weaker points and hone your good ones. It is not always easy to know when to struggle on bravely and when to change direction, but you will impress your hosts if you are willing to confront issues head-on, discuss matters openly and make adjustments as necessary.

> **Strengthening practice**
>
> Ensure that you demonstrate an informed sort of determination and not an impetuous one.

Satisfy the host teacher

When teachers agree to receive trainees into their classrooms, they always hope fervently for a 'good' one, by which they mean that the trainee is confident, competent and creative. Teachers also want people who are earnest about the job without being solemn, have a relaxed manner around other adults without being flippant, and relate well to pupils without being immature. If you are a bit weak in some of these departments, don't be anxious; every experienced teacher was once in your position and most of them remember all too well the mixture of fear and excitement that accompanies a fresh experience in school. On the other hand, don't confuse teachers' cheerful welcome and reassuring manner with a lack of seriousness about their role in helping you to adjust to the demands of teaching and fulfilling the requirements that result in a successful placement. For your part, you must exhibit a sturdiness of will and resolute determination to succeed, while adopting a 'professionally relaxed' approach. Teachers are uncomfortable both with a trainee who is aggressively determined but also with one who is nervously passive.

> **Strengthening practice**
>
> Find the amusing side of situations; laugh when you can; and learn as much as you can, whenever you can, from whomever you can.

Analyse and reflect on practice

New teachers are not only expected to do the things that are required of them but also to probe the *reasons* for doing something in a particular way and consider alternative approaches over time. Evaluating your practice consists of six components, each of which begins with the letter R:

1   *Rehearsing* in your mind the key elements of the lesson or session.
2   *Recalling* key decisions that you had to make.
3   *Retracing* the way that you introduced and developed the lesson.
4   *Rectifying* any limitations in your lesson plan that became apparent.
5   *Respecting* the fact that you still have much to learn about the job.
6   *Reminding* yourself that you did lots of things well.

REHEARSING

Scan the lesson as if you were an objective onlooker. It helps to make a simple diagram of the session to ascertain its *shape* (how much time and energy you devoted to which bits) and the *pattern of events* (the procedures and pupil responses).

RECALLING

Note two or three *critical moments* when you had to make spontaneous decisions, and consider whether you would do the same again or, if not, what alternative action was preferable.

RETRACING

Evaluate the lesson's effectiveness by retracing your steps under four headings: (a) Clarity of your explanation, (b) Relevance of your teaching methods and resources, (c) Quality of your communication with children and assistants, (d) Nature and effectiveness of the pupil learning.

RECTIFYING

Annotate your lesson plan to show where it might have been improved with particular attention to personalised learning (see Chapter 5).

RESPECTING

Write down a few questions about aspects of teaching for which you will seek advice from respected colleagues and do so as soon as possible.

REMINDING

Make an effort to 'pat yourself on the back' for successfully negotiating the lesson and relish the satisfaction.

Terminology

Evidence is information gathered systematically and offers insights and perspectives that are useful to take into account when making decisions about teaching and learning.

Proof is irrefutable, undeniable fact that leads to an inevitable conclusion about the right way to proceed.

Strengthening practice

Analyse in such a way that you can celebrate your achievements before addressing your limitations.

Accept advice thoughtfully

The main responsibility of host teachers and tutors is to the pupils in their charge but they also have a responsibility towards you, the trainee. You, in turn, have a responsibility to yourself, but also to the staff and pupils in the placement school. It's a two-way process that is intended to benefit both you and the school. You bring your enthusiasm, new ideas and energy to the staff and pupils; the teachers and assistants bring experience, opportunities and resources from which you can draw and learn. When host teachers make it perfectly clear that you must do such and such, your responsibility is to comply with as much enthusiasm as you can muster. On other occasions the teacher or tutor will advise but not insist; they may be unsure about what is best or want you to grapple with an issue rather than be told. You may be also offered options such that you have a stark choice. See below for a sample list of those occasions when you must do as you are told unquestioningly and those occasions when you may be given a choice of options. To discover the status of the advice that you are given, put your decision to the person concerned for their verification. If the person insists that it is up to you, then you make the final decision; if the person hesitates or enthuses about your choice, you can be sure that the teacher or tutor holds a strong preference for one option. Whatever the outcome, aim to do six things at least:

1   Thank the teacher for the advice.
2   Explain how and when you intend to implement it.
3   Ask if the teacher will monitor what you do and provide feedback.
4   Review the success of the strategy over a period of (say) a week.
5   Discuss with the teacher how you might further develop the strategy.
6   Keep a brief written record for future reference of: (a) the issue (b) the strategy (c) the outcome (d) the implications for the future (e) your review meeting with the teacher or tutor.

FORMS OF ADVICE

Advice is a *requirement* when:

* it is a directive based on school policy
* the children are used to working in that way

- a group of teachers have agreed between themselves on the right course of action
- the teacher or tutor says that she or he will observe you in action to see how you implement the advice.

Advice is a *choice* when:

- you are introducing a new curriculum theme that requires exploration
- it is a one-off lesson or session without future implications for deep learning
- you are carrying out a directed task as part of your course of study
- you receive the advice from a substitute teacher or TA.

Extra-curricular opportunities

In the UK there has been an explosion of initiatives for under-5s, expansion of before-school and after-school provision and use of school buildings for the local community (e.g. parenting classes; keep-fit; local history). Some schools are also involved in educating and informing parents about (for instance) the teaching of reading, number and a Modern Foreign Language (MFL) (see Martin *et al.*, 2008). While your main responsibility as a trainee teacher is to prepare, teach, supervise and assess children's learning, involvement in other areas of school life allows you to experience more directly what it feels like to be a 'real' teacher, with the accompanying time pressures, expenditure of energy and fulfilment (see Chapter 2). The host teachers like to feel that you are willing to share the thrills and spills associated with teaching as a career and will welcome your offers to assist in, for example, a lunchtime sports' club or extra mathematics' coaching after school. In turn, you will benefit from observing at close quarters how qualified teachers handle out-of-class sessions in a more informal setting.

Extend your thinking

Your involvement with children in extra-curricular activities not only helps you to develop competence but also gives you something else to refer to when applying for a teaching post.

Excelling on school placement

There is a longstanding joke about a mother who is trying desperately to rouse her son out of bed, only to be met by a series of pitiful excuses from the reluctant sleeper that no one likes him and that 'they' are all out to get him. The joke turns on the fact that the son is, in fact, a teacher and not a pupil. Such dark humour appeals to people who work in school because the caricature contains a grain of truth about the tension between hope and despair in the job. There exists for teachers at every stage of their careers (from novice to seasoned 'pro,') a fine line between exhilaration and disappointment; satisfaction and dismay; confidence verging on arrogance and insecurity verging on paranoia. Every teacher reading this account will empathise with the interwoven and sometimes bewildering blend of emotions with which each practitioner is grappling. Like Charles Dickens' ghost of *Christmas Yet to Come*, they constitute an unseen presence that will not speak its name.

Extend your thinking

You may hear or read that true professionals are able to set aside their emotions and just get on with the job. This 'instrumental' view of a teacher's role sits uneasily with plenty of evidence showing that the professional and personal dimensions are inseparable.

Your own beliefs about how you are progressing as a teacher are important in providing reassurance that all is well and that you are not going to be suddenly asked to leave the school! The single most important person with respect to determining your progress is the supervising tutor who formally observes your lessons and decides if you have met the required standard for that particular experience in school. Put starkly, if the tutor is satisfied, you can relax; if not, the situation becomes complicated and potentially stressful for you. You will be pleased to hear that the vast majority of trainees are successful; however, there are always issues to deal with and, as described in the previous chapter, dilemmas and challenges to face and overcome.

Successful trainee reports

The vast majority of trainee teachers successfully complete their school placements and receive due credit for all their efforts. There follow some genuine extracts from summary reports that tutors have written about the trainee teachers they have supervised. First, an extract from a tutor's report on Nathan, who was not endowed with a lot of natural talent but compensated for it by working diligently:

> Nathan has worked very hard throughout this school experience. He has shown true professionalism and been a welcome addition to the school staff. He uses his own initiative in the classroom and has been very efficient in his planning and execution of the curriculum. Nathan has

proved himself to be reliable, committed to encouraging the children to succeed and diligent in his preparation for the class in general. He has responded to advice and guidance, and has used ideas in planning for future lessons. Nathan has taken every opportunity to be involved in staff training and taken an active part in discussions during team meetings.

Note some of the key phrases used in this section of the report:

- worked very hard
- shown true professionalism
- very efficient
- committed to encouraging
- responded to advice
- every opportunity to be involved
- active part.

Mervyn was a mature trainee, whose report reflects his natural abilities and willingness to use them for the children's benefit. Like Nathan, he was also receptive to advice and willing to be involved beyond the confines of the classroom. Thus:

> Mervyn's success is due primarily to the fact that he has worked consistently hard throughout his time with us, seeking advice and using it to improve his teaching ability for the benefit of the children. His thoroughly professional approach has enabled him to establish effective relationships with colleagues and children. He has made valuable contributions to the wider life of the school by volunteering to help with an after-school club as well as participating wholeheartedly in the class residential visit.

Not surprisingly, Mervyn was offered a job at that very school. Although Mervyn and Nathan had different personalities – Nathan was highly strung, a bit impulsive and desperate to please, while Mervyn was calm and quietly confident – and were teaching different ages and placed in different types of schools, they were commended in similar ways by the two tutors for their consistent effort throughout the time on placement, determination to contribute wholeheartedly and willingness to take and act upon advice. Two further extracts from tutors about two other trainees, Paris and Melissa, make similar points but stress their relationships with pupils more heavily. Thus, for Paris, the tutor wrote:

> Throughout the practice you have demonstrated strength, determination and a desire to give the children the best experience you could offer. This class has had little opportunity in developing independent thinking skills; you strove to give them that opportunity, and succeeded. You also

developed effective behaviour management strategies and in setting up a rewards system you gained the children's respect and understanding. Your use of IT to support your teaching and enhance children's learning struck the balance between providing information and sparking pupil imagination. Their growing enthusiasm was clearly evident across the weeks of the placement.

By contrast, Melissa did not possess the same intellect as Paris but persevered to ensure that her relationship with the children was of such quality that their motivation to learn remained consistently high. Thus:

> Melissa has presence in the classroom, develops good professional working relationships with children and with other adults in the school. Her planning, teaching and assessment are all of high quality, and she soon became a valuable member of the teaching staff. Melissa has high expectations of pupils, too; even though she is quick to praise and value good work, she also sees where improvements can be made and supports pupils in achieving them. A particular strength of Melissa's is the way she established a rapport with her class, who responded to her calm, unfussy and clear expectations with good behaviour and enthusiastic working.

Melissa's school experience was characterised by many of the qualities mentioned above for the other three trainees and the tutor appears to have been particularly impressed by four aspects of Melissa's work:

1   her high expectations of pupils
2   her readiness to praise genuinely good work
3   her readiness to point out where work could be improved
4   her steady approach, leading to good behaviour and enthusiastic working.

Finally, imagine receiving a report from your tutor that read like the one below for Grace:

> Grace's classroom management was positive and sensitive. She got to know each child intimately and catered for individual needs extremely well. Grace was able to use her excellent knowledge of the children to plan appropriately, ensuring that their style, interests and responses were met. She challenged herself to have a go and pushed herself outside her comfort zone. She asked questions when appropriate and was not slow in seeking the advice of other professionals. Grace was an excellent example of resourcefulness, resilience, reciprocity and reflectiveness. She took on board and put into practice the notion of child observation to inform her assessment for the next learning steps. She used effective assessment for learning and kept realistic and workable assessment records, which she has used to

inform her planning. Grace has all the qualities to become an excellent teacher with her joyful disposition and positive nature contributing so well to the learning environment. Grace is easy to work with; she contributes her ideas, values all the pupils in class and has a delicious sense of humour.

Extend your thinking

Take every training and learning opportunity available, both in the placement school and, where possible, in other affiliated schools.

Strengthening practice

Write down the key characteristics identified by the tutor in Grace's report and consider your own progress against them. What qualities do you possess or have the potential to develop that are not mentioned above?

Professional learning perspectives

School culture

A generation ago, Bullough (1987) drew attention to the complexity of the social situation into which a new teacher is entering and the importance of sensitivity to the norms and values that define the school. Thus:

> When a beginning teacher enters school for the first time, s/he enters more than a building; s/he enters a culture of teaching that has evolved in response to school structure and wider cultural values that establishes what is the appropriate teacher role. To function successfully within the school, the beginning teacher must come to terms with this role and the values that sustain it. (p. 83)

Transition from novice to expert teacher

In her edited book about beginning primary teaching and learning, Moyles (2008) describes the transition between being a novice teacher and an expert teacher as being a steep one, not least because of the ever-changing face of primary education and new initiatives. Thus:

> In any profession, the learning curve between a state of being a novice and that of being an expert … is inevitably steep because there are always so many new issues to deal with simultaneously. Even when a certain level of

expertise has been gained, new initiatives often challenge existing securities. Whatever apparently rigorous and difficult roles people have had in previous experiences, entrants to the teaching profession ... may suddenly find themselves confronted with an overload of challenges. Because foundation stage and primary education concerns birth to 11-year old children ... these challenges are nearly always immediate and unrelenting: the children just do not go away while we get our act together! What needs to be acknowledged is that, with support and encouragement from others, the vast majority of people succeed as effective teachers and thoroughly enjoy their vocation. (p. 2)

Find out more by reading

Denby, N. (2008) *Gaining Your QTS*, London: Sage.
Hughes, P. (2008) *Principles of Primary Education*, 3rd edn, London: David Fulton.

Part 4

Achieving excellence

Chapter 10

Consolidating your professional learning

The content of Chapter 10 consists of:

- ways to identify gaps in your learning and enhance areas of strength
- prompts to stimulate deeper levels of engagement with key educational issues
- links with the Q-Standards for Qualified Teacher Status.

Points to consider as you read this chapter:

1 The need to constantly evaluate and refine your practice.
2 The implications of each exercise for your teaching competence and educational priorities.

Professional development

One of the fascinating aspects of being a teacher is that no matter how talented and committed you are, regardless of how much effort you are prepared to make, and no matter what status you attain, there is always room for improvement and parts of the job that you never fully master. It has become commonplace to classify teachers' progress under the descriptor *professional learning* and there is an expectation that all teachers will endeavour to enhance their knowledge of the curriculum, teaching methods and innovative practice.

The exercises that follow focus largely on general teaching competence (pedagogy) and do not deal specifically with subject knowledge or expertise. They provide you with a range of pragmatic issues to prioritise and make decisions about. The Q-numbers refer to the standards for Qualified Teacher Status in England and Wales and are not specifically relevant to readers outside those two countries.

Exercise 1 The purpose of education

(See standard Q3)

Circle one answer from the options provided:
AS = Agree strongly A = Agree NS = Not sure D = Disagree
DS = Disagree strongly

The purpose of education is:

1	To inculcate children into adult values	AS	A	NS	D	DS
2	To bring about economic prosperity	AS	A	NS	D	DS
3	To make good citizens	AS	A	NS	D	DS
4	To pass national tests	AS	A	NS	D	DS
5	To foster compliance in pupils	AS	A	NS	D	DS
6	To promote social cohesion	AS	A	NS	D	DS
7	To help children read and write	AS	A	NS	D	DS
8	To develop the whole person	AS	A	NS	D	DS
9	To prepare for secondary school	AS	A	NS	D	DS
10	To ensure a fairer society	AS	A	NS	D	DS

What do your decisions indicate about your educational priorities?
Summarise in your own words what it means to be a well-educated child.

Exercise 2 Teacher attributes

(See Q1, 2, 4, 5, 25)

Describe the attributes of a good teacher you have known or been taught by (preferably in primary school). You might wish to mention:

- characteristics that most impressed you about that person
- the values that appeared to underpin her/his actions as a teacher
- an example of where you saw the teacher exhibit these qualities.

Consider how you might incorporate her/his best practice in your own teaching.
    What specifically have you learned from this teacher about the art of teaching?

Exercise 3 Teacher values, attitudes and behaviour

(See Q2, 30)

- Give an example of a positive teacher value. How might it be expressed in the classroom?
- Give an example of a positive teacher attitude. How might it be expressed in the classroom?

- Give an example of positive teacher behaviour. How might it be expressed in the classroom?

Which of the following three descriptions best fits your beliefs about relationships in teaching?

1 I place a heavy emphasis upon my relationship between my pupils and me as a way to enhance quality of teaching and learning.
2 I believe in keeping something of a 'distance' between myself and the pupils to prevent them taking advantage of me.
3 I am looking for a good relationship but not at any price.

What are the implications of your beliefs for classroom practice?

Exercise 4 Teacher expectations

(See Q1, 18)

Offer a thoughtful response to each of the following statements ...

1 What do you mean when you refer to 'high expectations'?
2 How will you best transmit your own expectations to pupils?
3 What factors might hinder a pupil fulfilling his or her expectations?
4 How will you determine whether expectations are being met?
5 What part should children play in determining the expectations?

Exercise 5 Identifying learning objectives

(See Q22, 25b)

Which of the following constitute satisfactory lesson objectives and why/why not? Use the following questions to guide your thinking: (a) Is the objective rooted in the content of official documentation (NC/Primary Framework)? (b) Is the objective specific and realistically focused (or too vague)? (c) How easy will it be to evaluate learning outcomes?

1 to count in tens from zero to one hundred
2 to complete an activity sheet of addition sums
3 to understand the difference between adverbs and adjectives
4 to find information about Ghana from electronic sources
5 to draw sequential 'cartoon' pictures to illustrate events in the life of Oliver Cromwell
6 to give correct change and buy items using real money
7 to practise spelling oi, oa and ir words
8 to use a writing frame to write a letter to a school governor

9 to sort materials into categories of wood, paper and plastic
10 to be able to write and recognise simple words beginning with the letter 's'
11 to use capital letters and full stops correctly
12 to perform a song with actions linked to the music beat
13 to use small games equipment safely
14 to collaborate with other children in making a tall tower using paper and glue.

Exercise 6 Lesson schedules

(See Q 25a, 25b, 25c, 25d)

Using the 26-point lesson schedule (see below) respond to each point, based on a lesson that you have taught or observed. The lesson can be from any area of the curriculum. Do not confuse *objectives* (what you are trying to achieve) with the *methods* for achieving them (e.g. the tasks the children undertake during the lesson).

1 How many and how old were the children?
2 Where was the lesson in the overall sequence? (e.g. the first of a series, a one-off …)
3 How long was the lesson intended to last (and how successfully did you manage the time)?
4 What were the principal learning objective(s) and the subsidiary objective(s) for the lesson?
5 What tasks/activities were associated with achieving this/these objectives?
6 Where did the lesson 'fit' within the National Curriculum or Foundation Stage?
7 What did the children need to know and understand before they could engage with the lesson content?
8 What resources were needed, including ICT?
9 How did the lesson begin? (NOTE. The importance of engaging the children's interest.)
10 What was the overall lesson pattern? (e.g. introduction, teacher talk, division into ability groups, tasks and activities, lesson review.)
11 What sorts of questions were employed and what purpose did they serve?
12 Were the children divided into groups at any point? If so, on what basis?
13 To what extent were the children required to find out things for themselves?
14 What was the key vocabulary for the lesson and what other key words emerged?
15 How much time was spent on directly teaching the whole class?
16 What was done to monitor the children's understanding of the work and their progress?

17 What form of differentiation was used to match ability with task?
18 How were children who hurried to finish their work dealt with?
19 How were the more able pupils extended?
20 How were the less able pupils encouraged?
21 How much time was needed for clearing up, and how were the children and TA involved?
22 What assessment of children's progress took place?
23 What links were created between this lesson and the next steps?
24 What homework was set as a result of the lesson?
25 What was formally recorded about children's progress as a result of the lesson?
26 What is your overall impression of the lesson's quality? On what basis have you formulated your views?

Exercise 7 Teaching approaches

(See Q7, 10, 25a, 30, 31)

To what extent do the following statements most closely represent your teaching approach: (a) during literacy lessons, (b) during mathematics lessons, (c) during physical activity lessons, (d) during topic sessions?

Pupil involvement

1 I want my pupils to be actively involved in their learning as much as possible.
2 I want my pupils to be thinking deeply so that learning is more than surface deep.
3 I want my pupils to be responsive and offer their own opinions.

Pupil autonomy

1 I like my pupils to make their own decisions as often as possible to foster independence.
2 I believe that it is my responsibility to make most of the decisions in the classroom.
3 I think that pupils should make some decisions, but I have the final say.

What percentage of a typical lesson is occupied by you talking? What does this fact say about your teaching?

Exercise 8 Helping pupils to think for themselves

(See Q6, 10, 25b, 28)

By reference to the list of skills below, consider how successful you have been in promoting these qualities in your pupils by scoring each of the aims between 1 and 10, where 1 = 'not yet engaged with' and 10 = 'fully met'.

1   to work independently
2   to work as a member of a team
3   to listen respectfully to those who hold a different opinion
4   to understand the nature of a problem and be able to explain it to others
5   to extract key points from a mass of information
6   to ask probing questions that help to clarify an issue
7   to talk to others about reaching a correct decision
8   to persuade others about a particular position or idea
9   to summarise complex information into logical categories
10 to generalise from lots of specific instances (think inductively)
11 to identify how a general principle applies to a particular instance (think deductively)
12 to argue logically in promoting a belief or defending a decision
13 to interrogate and investigate a situation creatively in solving a problem (heuristic approach)
14 to draw reasonable conclusions from the available evidence.

List the areas that score 5 or under and draw up strategies for developing them.

Exercise 9 Responding to different contexts

(See Q8, 10, 25a, 25c, 25d)

Consider each of the following ...

1   The strategies you might employ to discover pupils' existing knowledge and understanding of sentence structure with: (a) reception children, (b) a class of eight year olds, (c) a class of eleven year olds.
2   State three factors you will take into account when planning a large-space lesson (e.g. PE, drama) with a village school class that consists of children from every year of Key Stage 2.
3   What strategies might you use to promote collaboration with pupils who are used to working independently?
4   How might your literacy teaching be different with and without the availability of TAs?

Exercise 10 Lesson evaluations

(See Q12, 22, 27, 28)

Consider a lesson that you have taught or observed recently and evaluate the eighteen statements (below) using the following scale:

1 = very weak
2 = weak
3 = satisfactory
4 = strong
5 = excellent

In doing so, consider (a) the criteria that you use to make your judgement and (b) what could be done to improve weaker areas.

1   Lesson intentions were clear.
2   Lesson intentions were communicated to the children.
3   Resources were available and accessible.
4   The lesson began positively and engaged the children's interest.
5   The teacher/you used a natural and enthusiastic voice.
6   Tasks and activities were explained fully and clearly to the children.
7   Tasks and activities were appropriate for the children.
8   The teacher/you were pleasantly firm and insistent.
9   The teacher/you dealt effectively with inappropriate behaviour.
10 The teacher/you monitored the children's learning carefully.
11 The teacher/you intervened and offered appropriate support.
12 The lesson concluded positively.
13 Complete and incomplete work was dealt with efficiently.
14 Children were given feedback about their progress.
15 Children were given opportunity to share with others what they had learned or experienced.
16 The teacher/you mentioned links with future lessons.
17 Resources were returned and the room left in good order.
18 Children were dismissed in an orderly manner.

The most memorable part of the lesson was ...
I learned that ...

Exercise 11 Using adult support

(See Q5, 20, 32, 33)

Examine the list of tasks below and produce an amended list of ten that are most relevant to assistants in primary schools ...

 1   collecting money
 2   chasing absences
 3   bulk photocopying
 4   copy typing
 5   producing standard letters
 6   producing class lists
 7   record-keeping and filing
 8   classroom display
 9   analysing attendance figures
10   processing exam results
11   collating pupil reports
12   administering work experience
13   administering examinations
14   invigilating examinations
15   administering teacher cover
16   ICT trouble-shooting and minor repairs
17   commissioning new ICT equipment
18   ordering supplies and equipment
19   stocktaking
20   cataloguing, preparing, issuing and maintaining equipment and materials
21   taking minutes at meetings
22   co-ordinating and submitting bids
23   seeking and giving personnel advice
24   managing pupil data
25   inputting pupil data.

For each of the ten selected statements indicate which adult is probably best suited to fulfil the role, using the following key:

TA   = teaching assistant
SNA = special needs assistant (responsible for a designated child)
LSA = learning support assistant (working alongside the teacher to raise standards of pupil attainment)
PV   = parent volunteer.

Exercise 12 Behaviour and discipline

(See Q2, Q10, Q31)

Examine your attitude to behaviour and discipline by answering the following questions:

1   What proportion of children behave well all of the time and most of the time?
2   When does most misbehaviour occur?
3   What sort of behaviour irritates you as a teacher and how do you deal with the emotions you experience?
4   How much do you agree that teachers can be too friendly with children?
5   How much do you agree with the argument that the very best teachers do not need to use extrinsic rewards (stickers, stars, etc.) because the children in their class are self-motivated?

Offer a brief response to the following ...

1   Describe two key strategies to promote a relaxed and purposeful learning climate, while ensuring that the children are well behaved.
2   List three principles you want to apply in maintaining good discipline among older primary children without being punitive.
3   It pays to start by being tough, as you can ease up later.

Exercise 13 Assessment

(See Q11, 12, 26a, 26b, 27)

You are handed a piece of children's written work to assess. What information would you want to know about the child, the work and the circumstances in which it was produced before assessing it?

Now consider the following ...

1   What are the links between AFL and AOL?
2   What factors determine whether teachers intervene or allow children to sort out problems for themselves?
3   How do we allow for the fact that some children remember something one day and forget it the next?
4   When offering feedback, is it ever relevant to give children unqualified praise? If not, why not? If so, why?
5   What are the advantages and limitations of setting individual pupil targets?
6   Evaluate the statement that 'records of pupil progress do not reveal the whole truth about attainment'.
7   When reporting to parents, what do we need to know about children other than their test scores?

Exercise 14 Every child matters

(See Q18, 21)

Drawing from the *Every Child Matters* (DfES, 2004) and other sources as appropriate, comment on one implication for your work as a teacher for each of the five sub-headings in each National Curriculum subject and RE.

Note: An 'implication' is what you will actively *do* as a result.

1   Being healthy
IMPLICATION:

2   Staying safe
IMPLICATION:

3   Enjoying and achieving
IMPLICATION:

4   Making a positive contribution
IMPLICATION:

5   Achieving economic well-being
IMPLICATION:

Make a list of other professionals who might be involved in providing support for vulnerable children in *each* of the five areas.

Exercise 15 SEN Code of Practice

(See Q19, 20, 25a)

Use the Code of Practice document to ascertain the following ...

1   the Code's central principles (see section 5.23)
2   the fourfold assessment process for primary children (5.6)
3   the fivefold approach that a school must adopt for children already identified with special educational needs (5.10)
4   the special circumstances pertaining to children for whom English is an Additional Language (5.16).

Exercise 16 Reporting to parents

(See Q4, 5)

Q4 states that trainees should be able to communicate effectively with children, young people, colleagues, parents and carers. Q5 states that trainees should be able to recognise and respect the contribution that colleagues, parents and carers can make to the development and well-being of children and young people, and to raising their levels of attainment. With these points in mind:

1   Mentally list three occasions when you can communicate informally with parents.
2   Ask a parent friend outside school what teacher attributes and attitudes impresses her/him.
3   Consider what you would say if a parent asked how she might best assist her five-year-old child and ten-year-old child at home.
4   Imagine that the host teacher asks you to help her in preparing for a parents' evening. Write a list of things you would want to know from the teacher in advance of the evening.

Exercise 17 Homework and out-of-class learning

(See Q24)

Consider the value and disadvantages of the following homework tasks in extending and consolidating learning. In your evaluation consider (a) the time it will take; (b) the ease with which it is manageable for the child; (c) the way it will be monitored and reviewed in class.

1   learning a list of random spellings
2   learning spellings embedded in a written passage
3   doing a set of sums of increasing difficulty
4   completing an unfinished self-portrait work from the lesson
5   finding out information from an Internet source
6   finding out information by asking parents and friends
7   drawing and sketching items of interest
8   writing a short fiction story
9   trying a simple experiment using common and safe household items
10   reading several pages of a 'reading' book
11   learning a short poem off by heart
12   monitoring eating habits over a week.

Exercise 18 What the experts say

(See Q7, 8, 9)

The following quotations are intended to stir, guide and inspire you. For each quotation:

- indicate how much you agree with the statement by using: C = completely agree; P = partially agree; N = do not agree
- frame one question you would like to ask the author
- consider the implications for your professional development ...

Chaplain, R. (2003) *Teaching without disruption in the primary school*. London: Routledge: 'During the initial interactions with pupils or whole classes you will automatically make rapid assessments of them. If you couldn't make assessments of your pupils, you wouldn't be doing your job' (p. 41).

Charlton, T. (1996) 'Listening to pupils in classrooms and school', in Davie, R. and Galloway, D. (eds) *Listening to Children in Education*, London: David Fulton: 'Children stand to derive much from being listened to: their academic success can be improved, their personal problems can be reduced, their self-esteem and motivation can be enhanced' (p. 63).

Clouder, C. and Rawson, M. (2003) *Waldorf Education*, Edinburgh: Floris Books: 'Childhood is the most important time of our lives. In a person's life there is no more decisive phase for the development of the whole human being' (p. 20).

Cullingford, C. (1997) 'Assessment, evaluation and the effective school', in Cullingford, C. (ed.) *Assessment Versus Evaluation*, London: Cassell: 'The successful teacher, for instance, will be fair and consistent, will praise more than blame, will be clear and patient, will ask questions and listen, rather than shout and present repetitive exercises' (p. 113).

Denby, N. (2008) 'Qualifying to teach: an introduction', in Denby, N. (ed.) *Gaining Your QTS*, London: Sage: 'When introducing yourself to a new class it is essential that you learn names. Children and young people respond much more readily when spoken to by name. You could make this part of a game or exercise, supply labels or make learners state their name before answering a question' (p. 4).

Fried, R. (1995) *The Passionate Teacher: A practical guide*, Boston: Beacon Press: 'To be a passionate teacher is to be someone in love with a field of knowledge, deeply stirred by issues and ideas that challenge our world, drawn to the dilemmas and potentials of the young people who come into class each day' (Prologue).

Hopkins, D. *et al.* (1997) *Creating the Conditions for Classroom Improvement*, London: David Fulton: 'It is generally accepted that effective classrooms are characterised by a positive working atmosphere, which includes an emphasis on celebrating achievement' (p. 44).

Katz, L. G. and Chard, S. C. (2000) *Engaging Children's Minds: The Project Approach*, Stamford: Ablex: 'When children are intrinsically motivated, they respond in ways that strengthen their disposition to work independently of the teacher; for example, by helping one another' (p. 14).

Killick, S. (2007) *Emotional Literacy at the Heart of the School Ethos*, London: Paul Chapman: 'The most valuable learning is often gained from painful errors and this learning is more likely enhanced if one is not left feeling attacked, humiliated or defensive' (p. 46).

Lawrence, D. (2006) *Enhancing Self Esteem in the Classroom*. London: Paul Chapman: 'Take your work seriously; but never take yourself seriously to the extent that you lose your sense of humour' (p. 97).

Lloyd, C. and Beard, J. (1995) *Managing Classroom Collaboration*, London: Cassell: 'Opportunities to listen to children talking in a variety of situations – alone, in groups, during problem-solving activities, in fantasy play, in the playground and in the structured classroom environment are a crucial part of assessment' (p. 6).

Richards, C. (2006) 'Primary teaching: a personal perspective', in Arthur, J., Grainger, T. and Wray, D. *Learning to Teach in the Primary School*, London: Routledge: '[Primary teaching is] an extremely complex activity … an amalgam of many elements: interpersonal, intellectual, physical, spiritual, even aesthetic … It involves notions such as respect, concern, care and intellectual integrity that are impossible to define but which are deeply influential in determining the nature of life in classrooms … It is a moral enterprise as well as a practical activity' (p. 13).

Roffey, S. and O'Reirdan, T. (2003) *Plans for Better Behaviour in the Primary School*, London: David Fulton: 'What we say and how we say it to children establishes and defines the quality of the relationship we have with them' (p. 22).

Smidt, S. (2006) *The Developing Child in the 21st Century*, London: Routledge: 'We see how children everywhere develop a range of strategies as problem-solvers, and in doing this make hypotheses, try these out, analyse what happens, identify patterns, generate rules, use analogy, come to conclusions and move on' (p. 107).

Find out more by reading

Arthur, J., Grainger, T. and Wray, D. (2006) *Learning to Teach in the Primary School*, London: Routledge.
Hayes, D. (2008) *Foundations of Primary Teaching*, 4th edn, London: David Fulton.

Conclusion
The wonder years of primary teaching

Being a teacher is a privilege and a responsibility: it is a privilege to have such close contact with developing young minds and active little people; it is a responsibility to realise that so many children, parents and members of the community depend on your skill, commitment and expertise. Not every child is a pleasure to work with but most are delightful; a few etch themselves in your memory and in those rare moments of contemplation in the coming years they will stand out like a beacon in your mind. Occasionally, a child brings you grief and may even cause you to despair. It is in times such as these that your motivation and determination are most severely put to the test and you recognise that the emotional dimension of teaching is every bit as important as practical skills and procedural niceties.

Every survey shows that people become teachers because they want to serve children and believe that education is a means to ensure a better society and happier world. Naturally, there are more practical benefits, such as (hard-earned) long holidays and some flexibility about arriving and leaving work. However, these pragmatic considerations are relatively minor in comparison with the vocational call of teaching and the pleasure of working alongside similarly committed adults in a school or educational setting.

We normally think of a 'calling' as something that only applies to people who choose religious or sacrificial ways of life; in fact, being a teacher can also be correctly referred to as a 'calling' because the good of others lies at the heart of the job. Those who are called to teach have a true vocation because they are on a mission to enable each child to maximise his or her talents, imagination, analytical skills and creativity, and to build strong character.

The greatest rewards of being a teacher have always been intrinsic ('within self'); most of the job satisfaction you experience comes from watching children grapple with and learn wonderful things, take journeys into the unknown, use their imaginations and discover a new world of knowledge and thought, as they suddenly grasp the meaning of a word, the logic of a mathematics problem, the significance of living things, the reality of other people's lives or the ways in which historical events relate to the present. Central to your vocation is to foster exhilaration for learning that cannot be easily measured or formally assessed but can be seen, felt, heard and experienced.

Teachers have been compared to gardeners, who plant thousands of seeds in the fertile earth: some germinate, others wither; most produce healthy plants; a few have stunted growth. You have the responsibility and pleasure of adding the 'fertiliser' to create a nurturing, learning climate that fans the strong breezes of motivation, invites the saturating rains of curiosity and initiates the warm sunshine of success to bring life to the seed, produce green shoots of growth and a proliferation of flowers. Listen to pupils' voices and childish chatter; enjoy their simple pleasures; celebrate small beginnings; be a guide and true educator to them. Make sure that your classroom is a joyful one, where children feel that learning is worthwhile and setbacks are but a temporary stumbling block on the road to victory.

Extend your thinking

You won't make a fortune by teaching and probably won't win a Teacher of the Year award; but you have the opportunity to win the hearts and minds of hundreds, perhaps thousands of children down the years, and win their undying gratitude.

Find out more by reading

Hayes, D. (2006) *Inspiring Primary Teaching*, Exeter: Learning Matters.
Scott, J. and Sornson, R. (1997) *Teaching and Joy*, Alexandria, VA: ASCD Publications.

References

Baines, E., Blatchford, P. and Kutnick, P. (2008) *Promoting Effective Group Work in the Classroom*, London: David Fulton.

Bullough, R. V. (1987) 'Accommodation and tension: teachers, teacher role and the culture of teaching', in Smyth, J. (ed.) *Educating Teachers: Changing the nature of pedagogical knowledge*, London: Falmer.

Caine, R. and Caine, G. (1994) *Making Connections: Teaching and the human brain*, New York: Addison-Wesley.

Chaplain, R. (2003) *Teaching without Disruption in the Primary School*, London: Routledge.

Cheminais, R. (2008) *Every Child Matters: A practical guide for teaching assistants*, London: David Fulton.

Coultas, V. (2007) *Constructive Talking in Challenging Classrooms*, London: Routledge.

Dalton, J. and Fairchild, L. (2004) *The Compassionate Classroom: Lessons that nurture wisdom and empathy*, Chicago: Zephyr Press.

Day, C. (2004) *A Passion for Teaching*, London: Routledge Falmer.

Day, C., Sammons, P., Stobart, G., Kington, A. and Gu, Q. (2007) *Teachers Matter: Connecting lives, work and effectiveness*, Maidenhead: Open University Press.

Department for Education and Skills (DfES) (2004) *Every Child Matters: Change for Children*, London: DfES.

Dix, P. (2007) *Taking Care of Behaviour*, Harlow: Pearson Education.

Eke, R. and Lee, J. (2008) *Using Talk Effectively in the Primary School*, London: David Fulton.

Fisher, R. (2005) *Teaching Children to Learn*, 2nd edn, Cheltenham: Nelson Thornes.

Franklin, S. (2006) 'VAKing out learning styles: why the notion of learning styles is unhelpful to teachers', *Education 3–13*, 34 (1), 81–7.

Galloway, J. (2007) *Primary ICT for Teaching Assistants*, London: David Fulton.

Gregory, E. (2008) *Learning to Read in a New Language*, 2nd edn, London: Sage.

Hall, K. (2007) 'Assessing children's learning', in Moyles, J. (ed.) *Beginning Teaching, Beginning Learning in Primary Education*, Maidenhead: Open University Press.

Hayes, D. (2004) 'Recruitment and retention: insights into the motivation of primary trainee teachers in England', *Research in Education*, 71 (May), 37–49.

Hoyle, E. (1969) *The Role of the Teacher*, London: Routledge & Kegan Paul.

Invernizzi, A. and Williams, J. (2007) *Children and Citizenship*, London: Sage.

Jacklin, A., Griffiths, V. and Robinson, C. (2006) *Beginning Primary Teaching*, Maidenhead: Open University.

Jeffreys, M. V. C. (1971) *Education: Its nature and purpose*, London: George Allen & Unwin.

Johnston, R. and Watson, J. E. (2007) *Teaching Synthetic Phonics*, Exeter: Learning Matters.

Jones, P. and Robson, C. (2008) *Teaching Music in Primary Schools*, Exeter: Learning Matters.

Kelly, P. (2005) *Using Thinking Skills in the Primary Classroom*, London: Paul Chapman.

Killick, S. (2007) *Emotional Literacy at the Heart of the School Ethos*, London: Paul Chapman.

Kohn, A. (2003) 'What does it mean to be well educated?' *Principal Leadership*, March, pp. 6–9.

Maddock, M., Drummond, M. J., Koralec, B. and Nathan, I. (2007) 'Doing schools differently: creative practitioners at work', *Education 3–13*, 35 (1), 47–58.

Martin, C., Bald, J. and Rumley, G. (2008) *Primary Languages: Effective learning and teaching*, Exeter: Learning Matters.

Medwell, J. (2007) *Successful Teaching Placement: Primary and Early Years*, Exeter: Learning Matters.

Moyles, J. (ed.) (2008) *Beginning Teaching, Beginning Learning in Primary Education*, Maidenhead: Open University Press.

Myhill, D. A. and Jones, S. (2006) 'She doesn't shout at no girls', *Cambridge Journal of Education*, 36 (1), 63–77.

Noddings, N. (1992) *The Challenge to Care in Schools: An alternative approach to education*, New York: Teachers College Press.

O'Quinn, E. and Garrison, J. (2004) 'Creating loving relations in the classroom', in Liston, D. and Garrison, J. (eds) *Teaching, Learning and Loving*, London: Routledge, pp. 49–64.

Pagett, L. (2007) 'The joy of learning poetry off by heart', in Hayes, D. (ed.) *Joyful Teaching and Learning in the Primary School*, Exeter: Learning Matters.

Pinder, R. (1987) *Why Don't Teachers Teach Like They Used to?* London: Hilary Shipman.

Roche, J. and Tucker, S. A. (2007) 'Every Child Matters: tinkering or reforming – an analysis of the development of the Children Act (2004) from an educational perspective', *Education 3–13*, 35 (3), 213–23.

Sammons, P., Day, C., Kington, A., Gu, Q., Stobart, G. and Smees, R. (2007) 'Exploring variations in teachers' work, lives and their effects on pupils', *British Educational Research Journal*, 33 (5), 681–701.

Schiller, C. (1979) *Christian Schiller: In his own words*, London: A & C Black.

Sedgwick, F. (2008) *100 Ideas for Developing Thinking in the Primary School*, London: Continuum.

Smidt, S. (2006) *The Developing Child in the 21st Century*, London: Routledge.

Tauber, R. T. (2007) *Classroom Management: Sound theory and effective practice*, 4th edn, Orlando: Harcourt Brace College Publishers.

Training and Development Agency (2007) *Professional Standards for Teachers (Qualified Teacher Status)*, London: TDA.

Troman, G. and Woods, P. (2000) 'Careers under stress: teacher adaptations at a time of intensive reform', *Journal of Educational Change*, 1 (3), 253–75.

Waller, W. (1932) *Sociology of Teaching*, London: John Wiley.

Winkley, D. (2002) *Handsworth Revolution: The odyssey of a school*, London: Giles de la Mare Publishers.

Woolley, H. (2007) *Inclusion of disabled children in primary school playgrounds*, National Children's Bureau, as part of the series, *Understanding Children's Lives*, Joseph Rowntree Foundation Report.

Index